The Personal Finance Cookbook

The Personal Finance Cookbook

Easy-to-Follow
Recipes to Remedy
Your Financial Problems

Nick Meyer, CFP®

WILEY

Published by John Wiley & Sons, Inc., Hoboken, New Jersey.
Published simultaneously in Canada.

For general information on our other products and services or for technical support, please contact our Customer Care Department within the United States at (800) 762-2974, outside the United States at (317) 572-3993 or fax (317) 572-4002.

Wiley also publishes its books in a variety of electronic formats. Some content that appears in print may not be available in electronic formats. For more information about Wiley products, visit our web site at www.wiley.com.

Library of Congress Cataloging-in-Publication Data is Available:

ISBN 9781394210299 (Paperback)
ISBN 9781394210312 (ePDF)
ISBN 9781394210305 (ePub)

Cover Design: Jon Boylon/Wiley
Cover Image: © ugurhan/Getty Images
Author Photo: Courtesy of the Author
SKY10062105_120823

This book is dedicated to you, the reader, for taking decisive action to improve one of the most intimidating and confusing aspects of your life: your finances. Future you will thank you.

Contents

About the Author   xi

Introduction   xiii

Chapter 1:   The Basics   1

1.1   How to Open a Checking Account   1

1.2   How to Open a High-Yield Savings Account   3

1.3   How to Build an Emergency Fund   5

1.4   How to Build a Bulletproof Budget   7

1.5   How to Calculate Your Net Worth   10

1.6   How to Calculate Your Financial Independence "Number"   12

1.7   How to Choose a Savings Rate Based on When You
Want to Retire   15

Chapter 2:   Investing in the Stock Market   19

2.1   How to Open a Brokerage Account   19

2.2   How to Open Roth and Traditional IRAs   23

2.3   How to Open a 401(k)   27

2.4 How to Change Brokers 29
2.5 How to Choose What to Invest In 32
2.6 How to Buy Your First Stock 36
2.7 How to Invest as a Kid (or for Your Kids) 39

Chapter 3: Credit 43
3.1 How to Decide When to Use a Debit Card vs a Credit Card 43
3.2 How to Open Your First Credit Card 47
3.3 How to Open Your Next Credit Card 51
3.4 How to Build Your Credit Score 54
3.5 How to Build Your Kid's Credit Score Before They Can Even Walk 56
3.6 Travel Hacking: How to Use Credit Card Rewards to Travel for Free (or at a Steep Discount) 59

Chapter 4: Debt 65
4.1 How to Differentiate Between "Good" and "Bad" Debt 65
4.2 The Debt Snowball Method: The Best Way (Behaviorally) to Pay Off Debt 68
4.3 The Debt Avalanche Method: The Best Way (Logically) to Pay Off Debt 71
4.4 How to Lower Your Interest Rate by Consolidating Debt 74
4.5 How to Qualify for a Debt Management Plan 76

Chapter 5: Big Purchases 79
5.1 How to Not Get Scr*wed When Buying a Car 79
5.2 How to Decide Between Leasing and Buying a Car 82
5.3 How to Ensure Your Wedding Doesn't Set You Back Years Financially 85
5.4 Pets: How Much They Cost and How to Save Money on Common Expenses 87

Chapter 6: College 91
6.1 How to Save Money on College While You're Still in High School 91
6.2 How to Apply for Grants 95
6.3 How to Apply for Scholarships 98
6.4 How to Make College a Good Investment 101
6.5 How to Use a 529 Plan to Save for Your Kid's College 105
6.6 How to Pay Off Your Student Loans 108

Chapter 7: Housing 113
7.1 Is It Better for You to Rent or Buy a House? 113
7.2 How to Tell If Rent/Your Mortgage Payment Is Too
Expensive for Your Income Level 116
7.3 How to Buy Your First House 118
7.4 How to Decide Between a 15-Year vs 30-Year Mortgage 121
7.5 How to Reduce Your Living Expenses by House Hacking 123

Chapter 8: How to Make More Money 129
8.1 How to Negotiate Your Starting Salary and Signing Bonus 129
8.2 How to Ask for a Raise 133
8.3 How to Maximize Your Employee Benefits 135
8.4 How to Raise Your Salary by Job-Hopping without
Ruining Your Reputation 139
8.5 How to Start a Side Hustle 142

Chapter 9: Taxes 149
9.1 How to Pay Taxes If You Have a Normal Job 149
9.2 How to Pay Taxes as a Business Owner, Independent
Contractor, or Freelancer 154
9.3 How Investments Are Taxed 160
9.4 How Tax Extensions Work and How to File Them 164
9.5 How Amended Tax Returns Work and How to File Them 168

Chapter 10: Retirement 173
10.1 How to Begin Drawing Your Social Security Benefits 173
10.2 How and When You're Required to Draw from
Your Retirement Accounts 176
10.3 How to Determine How Much You Should Spend
Each Year in Retirement 180
10.4 How to Roll Over Old 401(k)s to an IRA 183

Chapter 11: Charitable Giving 187
11.1 How to Report Charitable Donations on Your Tax Return 187
11.2 How to Open a Donor-Advised Fund for Tax-Advantaged Giving 190

Chapter 12: Insurance 197
12.1 How to Use an HSA as an Extra Retirement Account 197
12.2 How to Obtain Health Insurance When It Isn't Provided by
Your Employer (When Turning 26) 201

12.3   How to Use an HSA as an Extra Retirement Account   205
12.4   How to Obtain Homeowner's Insurance   210
12.5   How to Obtain Renter's Insurance   213
12.6   How to Obtain and Save Money on Car Insurance   216
12.7   How to Determine When You Need Life Insurance   221

Chapter 13: Passive Income   225
13.1   Why Passive Income Is the Best Form of Income   225
13.2   How to Earn Passive Income from the Stock Market   227
13.3   How to Earn Passive Income from Real Estate Investing   231
13.4   How to Earn Passive Income from Digital Products   236
13.5   How to Earn Passive Income from Affiliate Marketing   240

Index   245

About the Author

Nick Meyer, CFP®, also known as "NickTalksMoney" to his 1,500,000+ followers (at the time of this writing) across the major social media platforms, is an expert in a wide spectrum of personal financial topics. From taxes, to investing, to budgeting, it's hard to find a financial topic Nick can't teach you a thing or two about.

His interest in personal finance started at a young age. As the child of two postal workers, paychecks were consistent but didn't afford any room for error. Whenever an unexpected expense came up (car repairs, medical bills, or he and his brother begging for the latest Xbox), arguments and stress soon followed.

Nick was determined to learn the "money secrets" that seemingly worry-free, wealthier families knew, so his future family wouldn't grow up with the same financial stress that he did.

So he earned a bachelor's degree in finance from the University of Minnesota, started work as a financial and tax advisor for high net worth individuals (aka multimillionaires), and earned both the CERTIFIED FINANCIAL PLANNER™ and the Enrolled Agent professional designations.

After earning these professional designations and four years of working with multimillionaires, Nick realized that most of the smart financial decisions the rich make can be made by *anyone* regardless of income level or net worth.

So why isn't everyone making great financial decisions? Nick believes it's a lack of access to knowledge more than anything. Neither school nor his parents taught him about investing, credit building, or budgeting, and there's very little chance he ever would've learned these skills if he hadn't pursued the career path he did.

In order to democratize access to this information, Nick decided to leave his job to teach the *world*, not just those who could afford high-priced financial planners, how to win with money. He did so by posting videos that are both entertaining and educational on TikTok, YouTube, Instagram, and Facebook under the handle @nicktalksmoney.

Fast forward three years, and his videos have been viewed over 100 million times, he has accrued over 1,500,000 followers, he has appeared on nationally syndicated TV shows *NBC Evening News* and *Bloomberg Quicktake*, and he has been featured in publications like *CBS*, *Yahoo Finance*, and *Bloomberg*.

Learn more about Nick at www.nicktalksmoney.com or @nick talksmoney on social media, and join his email newsletter at www .nicktalksmoney.com/newsletter.

Introduction

The Problem

If there is *one* thing you should reasonably expect to learn about in school, it's money—how to manage it, make more of it, avoid losing it, and properly give it. Money impacts our relationships, stress levels, emotions, comfortability, social standing, and the legacy we leave for our children, but, as of June of 2023, only 21 US states have a fully implemented, statewide requirement that high school students take a personal finance class before they graduate. Makes sense, right?

For something that impacts literally *everybody's* lives, why doesn't school even teach us the basics: how to open a bank account, how and why we should build a good credit score, and how to invest in the stock market? According to Affirm, the average American worries about their finances six times per *day*. Wouldn't we be much better off if this brain power was instead directed toward solving the big problems of the world, or spending quality time with friends and family?

I sure think so, which is why, after spending four years as a financial advisor to the wealthy, I went all-in on creating approachable, entertaining, yet still educational, personal finance content on TikTok, Instagram, and YouTube under the handle NickTalksMoney. My ultimate goal is to increase financial literacy rates by making the usually bland, intimidating, but important topic of personal finance as fun and easily digestible as possible! That's exactly what this book aims to do as well.

The Solution: Your Personal Finance Cookbook

Listen, if this is the first money-related book you *ever* read, I wouldn't blame you. Who has the time to thumb through 300 pages of a "normal" personal finance book where 1) it almost feels like the author is talking down to you the whole time, and 2) they write at such a high level the average person could never hope to understand their message? Let's be honest, who even sets aside the time to read *any* type of book when you could instead sit down on the couch and get instant access to millions of movies, TV shows, and internet videos with the click of a button?

All of this is to say that I'm well aware that most people would rather not spend the fleeting couple of hours of free time they have each week, after putting their nose to the grindstone at work or school, to dedicate brain power to learn *anything*, let alone something as seemingly complex as personal finance. So in this book, I've taken out *all* the fluff (save for this intro), industry jargon, and complexity. In the same way that you don't need to know exactly how sugar and flour chemically bond to create cookies, you don't necessarily need to have an advanced knowledge of modern portfolio theory, tax code, or credit risk premiums to successfully manage your personal finances.

I built my following by providing short, actionable, entertaining finance tips: a cookbook-style format is the most efficient way to provide this same value in print.

A cookbook isn't something you sit down and read cover-to-cover. It's designed for short, yet very valuable, interactions. If you're looking for a recipe on how to make a specific Greek salad, you find the page numbers for the recipe in the table of contents, turn to those pages, and then read the complete ingredient list and cooking instructions for that dish. If you want to make a salad but are unsure of what type of salad you want to make, you can flip through the salad section of the cookbook until you find one that catches your eye. If you have no idea what you want to cook but know you want to cook something, you could flip through the entire book and find the recipes you want to try in the future.

That's exactly how I want this book to work. If there's a specific topic you could use help with, like getting started with investing, all you need to do is navigate to pages 19–41 and you'll find exactly what you need. Or, if you could use help with investing as a whole, you can browse every recipe in Chapter 1 and follow the ones that pertain to you, while skipping over sections (like credit, for example) that you feel more well-versed in. If you don't know what specifically you need help with but know that your finances as a whole could use a facelift, you could thumb through each page and find the recipes that would be most helpful for you.

This cookbook is full of easily digestible, standalone "recipes" for life's most common personal finance topics from investing, to credit, to buying a home, and much, much more. Each recipe generally includes:

- **Setup Time**: How much time you have to devote to completing the task up front
- **Maintenance Time**: How much time you have to dedicate each month/year to the task
- **Function**: What the recipe helps you do (make money, save money, pay the debt, etc.)
- **Essential Terminology**: A list of all terminology you need to know to complete and understand the task explained as simply as possible

- **Ingredient List**: A list of items you need to complete the task (computer, phone, spreadsheet, apps, bank account, money, etc.)
- **Recipe**: A step-by-step walk-through of how to complete the task
- **Recap**: A overview and list of important ideas to keep in mind

Don't get me wrong—reading this entire book from cover to cover would be a *great* use of your time. However, I realize that your time is valuable, so this book is just as useful as a guide you can pick up and reference when your situation calls for it. Need to know the smartest way to buy a car? Turn to page 79. Need to know how to open your first credit card? Turn to page 47. Need to know how to pay taxes? Turn to page 149.

For far too long, this sort of financial knowledge has been gatekept by society's elite: if you didn't have parents who were financially literate *and* willing to openly speak about finances, you were out of luck because school wouldn't teach you this stuff. Now, all the financial knowledge you could ever need is right at your fingertips; it's just up to you to put forth the small amount of effort required to start learning about it. This cookbook is designed to make that as easy as possible for you by breaking the most common personal finance topics down to their simplest forms.

Let's start cooking!

Chapter 1
The Basics

1.1 How to Open a Checking Account

Setup Time	Maintenance Time	Function
10–30 Minutes	N/A	Manage Money

Checking accounts are a (near) necessity if you want to participate in the financial system—they provide you with a place to receive direct deposits, make payments, and transfer money to your investment accounts.

Essential Terminology

Checking Account: A type of bank account that lets you deposit money and make payments. Checking accounts can be opened with both banks and credit unions. It provides you with tools like checks and debit cards to pay for purchases, while the bank keeps a record of your transactions—also known as a bank account or spending account.

Bank: A for-profit financial institution that helps people keep their money safe and provides services to manage their finances. It allows you to deposit and store your money into various types of accounts, like checking and savings accounts.

Credit Union: A not-for-profit financial institution that provides many of the same services as a bank but limits membership to a specific community (residents of a certain state, for example) or organization (charity, employer, etc.). Credit unions often provide better interest rates and lower fees because they prioritize the needs of their members over making profits.

FDIC Insurance: A government protection that insures up to $250,000 of your cash (or $500,000 if married) per account in the event of your bank's failure. NCUA Insurance is the government protection equivalent for credit unions.

Ingredient List

Required:

- Personal identification (such as a driver's license or passport)
- Social Security number or ITIN
- Proof of address (utility bill, rental agreement, etc.)

Optional:

- Computer or smartphone (or you could travel to a local bank/ credit union and open your account in person)

Recipe

1. Research and choose a bank or credit union to open your account with. In general, banks may offer more services but charge more fees/offer lower interest rates on savings balances than credit unions, and typically have a larger national presence. No matter the institution, I'd recommend finding a checking account that:
   a. Doesn't have a minimum balance requirement.
   b. Doesn't have monthly maintenance fees.
   c. Has an intuitive mobile app (mobile check depositing is also a huge plus).
   d. Has strong reviews for customer service.
   e. Is FDIC insured—this is a *requirement*.
2. Visit the website of the bank/credit union you chose (bank websites will end with ".com," while credit union websites will end with ".org") and find their online application.

3. Enter the necessary information (often: name, birthday, Social Security number/ITIN, address, phone number, email address, and citizenship status) and upload scans of necessary documents, like a driver's license (not always required).
4. Submit and wait for your application to be approved.
5. Make your initial deposit, and set up direct deposit (if you have a job).

Recap

1. Research and choose which bank/credit union you want to open a checking account with.
2. Complete their online application.
3. Fund your account and ensure you set up direct deposit so your paychecks are automatically sent to your checking account.

1.2 How to Open a High-Yield Savings Account

Setup Time	Maintenance Time	Function
10–30 Minutes	N/A	Save *and* Make Money

> Wow, I'm so excited that my savings account pays me 0.02% in interest per year!
>
> —*said nobody, ever*

The average savings account in the USA pays just a *0.40% interes* rate as of June 2023. This means, for every $1,000 in your account, you'd earn a whopping $4 in interest per year. High-yield savings accounts (HYSAs), as their name suggests, offer a much higher interest rate than that. How much higher? That depends on a number of factors (most notably the Federal Funds Rate), but as of today, a typical HYSA is offering more than ten times more interest than a "normal" savings account. They can afford to offer much higher rates (while receiving the same protections as normal savings accounts) because a majority of HYSAs are offered by online banks: so instead of using their earnings to pay for fancy buildings and thousands of staff, they can instead direct these earnings back to their customers in the form of higher interest rates.

Essential Terminology

High-Yield Savings Account (HYSA): A special type of savings account that pays you a much higher interest than a "regular" savings account. They are typically offered by online-only banks and come with the same security and protections as "regular" savings accounts. However, these interest rates aren't permanent (neither are "regular" savings account interest rates) and fluctuate depending on a number of factors.

FDIC Insurance: A government protection that insures up to $250,000 of your cash (or $500,000 if married) per account in the event of your bank's failure. NCUA Insurance is the government protection equivalent for credit unions.

Ingredient List

Required:

- Computer or smartphone
- Bank account
- Social Security number
- Personal identification (such as a driver's license or passport)
- Proof of address (utility bill, rental agreement, etc.)

Recipe

1. Research and choose a bank to open your HYSA with. You can find my favorite HYSA providers at nicktalksmoney.com/HYSA. Factors to consider when opening an account are:
   a. Interest rate—is it competitive with other HYSA providers?
   b. Fees—avoid accounts with maintenance fees, minimum balance fees, or transfer fees.
   c. Accessibility—if needed, how quickly can you withdraw your money?
   d. FDIC Insurance—this is a *requirement*.

2. Complete the online application with all necessary information (often: name, birthday, Social Security number/ITIN, address, phone number, email address, and citizenship status) and upload scans of necessary documents, like a driver's license (not always required).
3. Submit and wait for your application to be approved.
4. Make your initial deposit, and turn on recurring deposits if you want to automatically deposit money into this account every month.

Recap

1. Choose an HYSA provider covered by FDIC Insurance.
2. Submit an online application.
3. Once you're approved, make an initial deposit and use it to build an emergency fund.

1.3   How to Build an Emergency Fund

Setup Time	Maintenance Time	Function
20–45 Minutes	5–30 Minutes per Month	Save Money

If an unexpected car repair racked up a bill of $1,000, would you be able to cover this without accruing credit card debt? Statistics suggest that 57% of Americans would answer "no" to this question, which is why building an emergency fund (preferably held in a high-yield savings account) is so important. This is the foundation of your personal finances and should be built before attempting to grow your money through investing.

Essential Terminology

Emergency Fund: A sum of cash set aside for unexpected financial needs or emergencies, like medical expenses or car repairs. It provides a safety net, allowing you to handle unforeseen circumstances without having to borrow money or rely on credit cards. The general recommendation is to have between three and six months' worth of necessary expenses held in your emergency fund.

High-Yield Savings Account (HYSA): A special type of savings account that pays you a much higher interest than a "regular" savings account. They are typically offered by online-only banks and come with the same security and protections as "regular" savings accounts. However, these interest rates aren't permanent (neither are "regular" savings account interest rates) and fluctuate depending on a number of factors. See page 3 for the HYSA recipe.

Ingredient List

Required:

- Savings account (preferably high-yield)
- Savings goal

Recipe

1. Set a savings goal: The general guidance is to have an amount equal to three to six months' worth of necessary expenses set aside in your emergency fund. This means, if your baseline expenses (rent, bare minimum groceries, etc.) cost $1,000 per month, you'd want to save between $3,000 and $6,000 in your emergency fund. If you have a stable income and don't own many assets that could generate unexpected expenses (house, car, etc.), you may choose to stick with the lower end, and vice versa if you have an inconsistent income or a risk to incur a lot of unexpected expenses.
2. Determine where to keep your emergency fund: as discussed on page 3, high-yield savings accounts currently offer 10 times more interest than a typical savings account. With your emergency fund likely amounting to at least a couple thousand dollars, the amount of interest you could earn if it's held in an HYSA isn't negligible.
   a. My favorite HYSAs are listed at nicktalksmoney.com/HYSA.
3. Treat this as a necessary expense: Set up an automatic transfer of a fixed dollar amount from your checking account every pay period

until you reach your savings goal. This ensures you don't even get the chance to think about using this money for anything else.

4. Only use this for true emergencies: Once your emergency fund is fully funded, don't use it for anything but emergencies. If other large but unnecessary expenses, like concert tickets, come up, start separate savings buckets for them.

5. Continue to adjust based on lifestyle inflation: As the years go on, your necessary expenses will likely rise. Ensure your emergency fund balance rises to reflect this.

Recap

1. Set a savings goal for your emergency fund (usually equal to three to six months' worth of necessary expenses).

2. Open a high-yield savings account to keep your emergency fund in.

3. Set up automatic transfers each pay period into your emergency fund and only use it for true emergencies to ensure you reach your goal.

4. Adjust your emergency fund every year to reflect any increase in living expenses.

1.4   How to Build a Bulletproof Budget

Setup Time	Maintenance Time	Function
20–45 Minutes	5–30 Minutes per Month	Save Money

Ugh, budgeting sounds about as fun as hitting myself in the shin with a scooter.

— you, probably

Well, yeah, if you look at budgeting simply as a way to constrain your spending, it's not going to feel like the most fun thing in the world. However, when you look at budgeting for what it *actually* is:

a roadmap that ensures you direct your money in such a way that maximizes your happiness today while still making progress toward your big-picture financial goals, it becomes clear that budgeting (in some form) should be part of everyone's overall financial strategy.

Essential Terminology

50/30/20 Rule: This is a simple budgeting rule that states your after-tax income (how much money you take home each month) should be divided as follows: up to 50% for necessary expenses (housing, transportation, basic groceries, etc.), up to 30% for wants (entertainment, dining out, shopping, etc.), and at least 20% for savings, investments, or paying down debt.

Ingredient List

Required:

- Computer or smartphone
- Bank account
- Credit card statements (if any)

Optional:

- Spreadsheet budgeting template (mine is available at nicktalks money.com/budget)
- Mobile budgeting apps (my favorites are listed at nicktalks money.com/budgetapps)

Recipe

1. To make a realistic budget, you need to understand two things: how much money you *make* in a month and how much money you spend in a month. To find real numbers for each (I guarantee there will be some variances between perception and reality, especially for spending), review your past three months of bank statements and credit card statements (if you use a credit card).

Write down your average monthly income (after taxes), and divide each month's expenses into the following categories:

   a. Necessary expenses (housing, transportation, groceries, utility bills, etc.)

   b. Spending on "wants" (entertainment, dining out, leisure travel, clothes shopping, etc.)

   c. Money put toward saving, investing, or debt repayment

2. Immediately, you'll almost certainly find some "red flags" or items that you're spending more money on than the value you receive for them justifies. This could be unused subscriptions, your weekly brunch bills, or even a high monthly car payment. Simply identifying and consciously making an effort to curb some of this red flag spending is more than most will ever do budgeting-wise. So, if you don't want to be one of those people that tracks every dollar spent on a massive spreadsheet with hard caps on monthly spending limits per category, at least start with this.

3. If you do want to get a little more in-depth with your budgeting, you can use your spending data to build a budgeting framework. Divide each of your expense categories by your monthly income to see how your spending breaks down at a percentage level (for example, $2,000 in necessary spending / $4,000 in income = 50% of your income is spent on needs). Your goal, right away, should be to adjust your spending to fit within the 50/30/20 rule (see definition above). This is a great baseline budget to follow because, as you'll learn on page 15, saving/investing 20% of your income will allow you to retire at a "normal" retirement age after around thirty-seven years of work.

4. To automatically track your spending and make following your budget as easy as possible, I highly recommend downloading a budgeting app like the ones I list on nicktalksmoney.com/budgetapps. Budgeting apps typically link directly with your bank accounts and credit cards to automatically track and categorize your monthly spending, so you don't have to go through the work of manually tracking everything (which, let's be honest, 99% of us would be too lazy to do, rendering our budgets useless).

5. If you *are* someone who loves numbers and want to manually track your spending on a spreadsheet, you can download my budgeting spreadsheet at nicktalksmoney.com/budget. Manually tracking your expenses will ensure you're completely in tune with your spending, making you much more likely to actually follow your budget. However, this comes with the obvious downside of being too much of a time commitment for most people to follow through with.

Recap

1. Review your past three months of bank and credit card statements to determine how much you make and spend during an average month.
2. Identify spending "red flags," which are areas that you spend much more money on than the joy/value they provide you, and consciously make an effort to reduce spending in these areas.
3. Adjust your spending to try to fit within the 50/30/20 budgeting framework.
4. Automate spend tracking with a budgeting app (nicktalksmoney .com/budgetapps has a list of my favorites).
5. For those who love number crunching, manually track your spending with my budgeting spreadsheet at nicktalksmoney .com/budget.

1.5   How to Calculate Your Net Worth

Setup Time	Maintenance Time	Function
10 Minutes	5 Minutes per Month	Goal Setting and Tracking

"I just became a millionaire!" *your smart friend announces.*
"But you're a plumber, how did you make $1 million in a year?" *you say.*
"I didn't, my NET WORTH just reached $1 million," *your smart friend replies.*

When someone says they're a millionaire, or billionaire for that matter, they're not referring to the amount of money they make in a year, they're referring to their net worth. This is the most accurate way to track where you are financially, so it's something I'd recommend updating monthly.

Essential Terminology

Net Worth: The total value of all the things you *own* (cash, stocks, property, etc.) minus any debts you *owe* (credit cards, auto loans, mortgages, student loans, etc.).

Ingredient List

Required:

- Computer or smartphone (or a pen, paper, and a calculator if you're old school)

Optional:

- Net worth calculator spreadsheet (mine is available for free at nicktalksmoney.com/networth)
- Mobile budgeting apps (my favorites are listed at nicktalks money.com/budgetapps)

Recipe

1. Calculate your net worth using one of three methods:
   a. List the value of all your assets and the amount you owe on all liabilities on a piece of paper, sum the value of the assets, and subtract the value of the liabilities. Congrats, you just found your net worth!
   b. Use my free net worth calculator at nicktalksmoney.com/ networth to fill in the value of all your assets and the amount you owe on all liabilities, and the sheet will automatically calculate and track your net worth.
   c. Nearly all of the budgeting apps I've listed at nicktalksmoney .com/budgetapps have net worth tracking built in. Simply

enter your assets and liabilities and most of the apps will tell you your net worth, and some will even track it over time.

2. Analyze your net worth. What makes up the largest part of your net worth? Is it something singular like a house, so your entire net worth swings with the housing market? Or is it more diversified across a variety of stocks, properties, and cash? If you have a negative net worth, what is the most pressing piece of debt you need to take care of?

3. Track your net worth. On the first day of every month, make it a practice to calculate your net worth, and write this down next to the month/year (there's a table for this in my net worth calculator). This is one of the best methods to track your progress, plus it can be fun to look at your net worth progression over multiple years of progress.

Recap

1. Calculate your net worth (what you *own* minus what you *owe*).
2. Analyze the different components of your net worth to identify areas of improvement.
3. Update your net worth on the first day of every month, and keep track of these balances to track your progress.

1.6   How to Calculate Your Financial Independence "Number"

Setup Time	Maintenance Time	Function
5 Minutes	N/A	Goal Setting

Your entire perspective on personal finance will change when you realize retirement isn't an *age*, it's a *number*. Reaching age 65 doesn't (magically) mean that you'll have enough money saved and invested to retire. Conversely, reaching age 35 with enough money to sustain your lifestyle indefinitely means that you'll never *need* to work another day in your life, so you could retire a full thirty years before society's "standard" retirement age. Reaching financial independence early in life doesn't mean that you *have* to stop working; it simply allows you to choose spending your time however you see fit without money being a large determining factor. Do you want to quit your boring job and travel the world with your family? Do you enjoy your job, but want to cut back on your hours? Are you expecting a child and want to spend the first year or two at home with them? Achieving financial independence makes all of these things a lot easier to do because the income from your investments (stock appreciation, dividends, interest, etc.) is enough to sustain your lifestyle on its own.

Essential Terminology

Net Worth: The total value of all the things you *own* (cash, stocks, property, etc.) minus any debts you *owe* (credit cards, auto loans, mortgages, student loans, etc.).

Financial Independence: When you have enough money saved and invested to cover your living expenses indefinitely without needing to rely on a job for income.

The 4% Rule: A retirement planning rule of thumb that states that as long as you withdraw 4% or less of your total retirement fund balance per year to live off of, and your retirement funds are invested 75% in stocks and 25% in bonds, there's a 92% chance (https://www.forbes.com/sites/wadepfau/2018/01/16/the-trinity-study-and-portfolio-success-rates-updated-to-2018/?sh=23ac23246860) that you can live off your investments comfortably for at least forty years.

Ingredient List

Required:

- The calculator on your phone

Optional:

- My free net worth calculator spreadsheet (nicktalksmoney.com/ networth), which includes a section for calculating your financial independence number

Recipe

1. Roughly estimate how much you spend in a typical year. Ask yourself if this is the amount of money you see yourself spending per year in retirement; if not, adjust the number so it is.
2. Divide this number by 0.04 (aka 4%) to find your financial independence number! This is how much you need to invest in your retirement funds to (theoretically) never need to work again.
   a. Example: you're very frugal and estimate that you'll only need $40,000 per year in retirement. $40,000 / 0.04 = $1,000,000, meaning that you should aim for a net worth of $1,000,000 before you think about retiring.
   b. If this number feels scary to you, it'll feel a lot less scary once you realize that the Trinity Study (https://www .aaii.com/files/pdf/6794_retirement-savings-choosing-a-withdrawal-rate-that-is-sustainable.pdf), which created the 4% rule, has the *very* conservative assumption that you won't earn a single dollar in retirement outside of your investments. This means no side hustles, Social Security, or even part-time work. The reality is, if you retire during what are prime working years for most, there's a strong chance that you'll end up doing something to generate at least a little bit of income.
3. Use this number as a broad net worth goal, not a number that's set in stone. It'll give you a tangible goal to shoot for, but, in reality, there's a strong chance that your desired annual spending changes significantly between the time you set this goal and the time you actually reach it. Evaluate your financial independence number annually to account for these changes in expenses.

Recap

1. Divide your desired annual expenses in retirement by 0.04 to find your financial independence "number."
2. Use this number as a broad goal, but adjust it annually if your desired expenses change.

1.7 How to Choose a Savings Rate Based on When You Want to Retire

Setup Time	Maintenance Time	Function
15 Minutes	N/A	Goal Setting

It's not how much you make, but how much you keep.

—old saying

That's the reason why, as of December 2022, 51% of those earning $100,000+ per year reported living paycheck to paycheck (https://time.com/6263989/six-figures-inflation-income/#:~:text=In%20December%202022%2C%2051%25%20of,companies%20PYMNTS%20and%20Lending%20Club). It doesn't matter how much money you make if, every time you get a raise, you upgrade your lifestyle by buying a nicer car, fancier clothes, and a bigger house. This could lead you to being significantly less wealthy on paper than someone making half of what you do. This is why your savings rate is one of the largest determining factors of your net worth, and consequently, how soon you achieve financial independence.

Essential Terminology

Savings Rate: The portion of your income that you set aside for saving and investing. For example, a 10% savings rate would mean that, for every $1,000 you earn, $100 is saved and invested.

Net Worth: The total value of all the things you *own* (cash, stocks, property, etc.) minus any debts you *owe* (credit cards, auto loans, mortgages, student loans, etc.).

Financial Independence: When you have enough money saved and invested to cover your living expenses indefinitely without needing to rely on a job for income.

Ingredient List

Required:

- Computer or smartphone
- Access to the website: networthify.com/calculator/earlyre tirement
  - I'm not affiliated with Networthify, and their website tech- nically isn't required, but it reduces your time spent from minutes to seconds.

Recipe

Note: This recipe is best followed after calculating your financial independence "number" in Section 1.6.

1. Enter your after-tax income, savings, and expenses information into networthify.com/calculator/earlyretirement
   a. This calculator will show you how soon you're projected to retire based on your current savings rate.
   b. Key assumptions of the calculator:
      i. Your current annual expenses are equal to your expected annual expenses in retirement.
      ii. Your savings are invested in the stock market, with a very conservative rate of return assumption of 5% per year (the stock market has returned an average of over 10% per year since 1926 (https://www.officialdata.org/us/stocks/s-p-500/1926), but this low return takes into account taxes and inflation.

iii. You will never draw down your principal (the initial amount you invest); you'll only live off of the earnings from your investments.

iv. The income you enter is what remains after taxes.

2. If the "you can retire in" number is higher than you'd like, adjust the "current savings rate" variable until you find a retirement date you're comfortable with. Ensure your target savings rate is both sustainable and realistic; you want to balance living today while also saving for tomorrow. For examples of what different savings rates will get you, according to the calculator, see the following:

a. A 5% savings rate (the average American's savings rate in 2023) (https://www.cnbc.com/2023/04/27/us-personal-savings-rate-falls-near-record-low-as-consumers-spend .html#:~:text=Here's%20why,-Published%20Thu%2C%20 Apr&text=The%20U.S.%20personal%20savings%20 rate,continues%20and%20wage%20growth%20slows) would require you to work for nearly sixty-six years before you can retire.

b. A 10% savings rate (closer to the historical average for Americans) would require you to work for over fifty-one years before you could retire.

c. A 20% savings rate (which is recommended by financial planners) would let you hang up your hard hat after a little under thirty-seven years of work.

d. And, for the ambitious financial independence seekers (I count myself among them), a 50% savings rate should give you the option to retire after sixteen years of work.

3. This is the hard part: actually follow your savings rate target. To make this easier on yourself, set up automatic investments that pull money from your checking account each month and invest it.

a. To reduce the chance of you "accidentally" spending this money instead of investing it, make these automatic invest-ments occur as soon after you receive your paychecks as possible. For example: if you receive your paychecks on the 1st and 15th of each month, it would be good practice to set up your automatic investments on the 2nd and 16th of each month. This gives your deposits time to settle while ensuring you have little time to spend them elsewhere.

Recap

1. Enter your information into networthify.com/calculator/ear lyretirement.
2. Adjust the "current savings rate" variable to find a savings rate that fits your goals.
3. Follow this savings rate by putting automatic investments in place.

Chapter 2

Investing in the Stock Market

2.1 How to Open a Brokerage Account

Setup Time	Maintenance Time	Function
15 Minutes	N/A	Make Money

Investing in the stock market doesn't require you to call up a Wall Street trader or have any insider connections; all you need is a brokerage account. You can think of a brokerage account as a checking account that lets you invest in the stock market: you deposit money into the account, and instead of that money just sitting there, you can invest it into the stock market with just a couple of clicks on your computer or a couple of taps on your phone.

Essential Terminology

Brokerage Account: A non-retirement account that allows you to invest in stocks, bonds, index funds, ETFs, mutual funds, certificates of deposit, etc. There are no contribution, withdrawal, or income limits. Unlike retirement accounts, brokerage accounts do not offer tax-saving incentives for the money you deposit into them. They are free to open and don't have any ongoing account fees (at most major brokers).

Broker: It's a fancy way to refer to the company that hosts your brokerage account. Just as you associate "banks" like Chase, Wells Fargo, and Bank of America with checking accounts, you can associate "brokers" like Fidelity, Vanguard, and Charles Schwab with brokerage accounts. Brokers are specifically licensed to facilitate transactions on the stock market, whereas most "regular" banks aren't. Note that the brokers I discuss here are specific to the USA: each country generally has its own set of brokers, though there are some that operate in dozens, or even hundreds, of different countries. See a list of my favorite brokers, both US and non-US, at nicktalksmoney.com/investingapps.

Robo Advisor: A broker that automatically makes investments for you depending on how you answer a set of onboarding questions. This is a truly hands-off investing experience, but, unlike self-managed brokerage accounts, you will be charged a fee for this service.

SIPC Insurance: Government-provided insurance (you don't have to opt in or pay for it) that protects up to $500,000 of assets (stocks, bonds, cash, etc.) held in your brokerage account in the event of the broker's bankruptcy. This *doesn't* protect you from your stocks losing value due to fluctuations in the market; it's only when your assets are lost because your broker has failed (assuming they are an SIPC member). All brokers I list here have SIPC insurance. If you want to use another broker, ensure they are covered by SIPC insurance.

Ingredient List

Required:

- Computer or smartphone
- Personal identification (such as a driver's license or passport)
- Social Security number or ITIN
- Proof of address (utility bill, rental agreement, etc.)

Optional:

- My list of my favorite mobile-first brokers at nicktalksmoney
.com/investingapps

Recipe

1. Choose a broker. The major decision here is whether you want
to choose one of the older, more established brokers like Fidelity,
Vanguard, or Charles Schwab, go with one of the newer, mobile-
first brokers, or want the hands-off investing experience that
Robo Advisors provide. My thoughts on each category are below:
   a. The "Big 3" brokers, Fidelity, Vanguard, and Charles Schwab
      i. Positives: Not only do they offer brokerage accounts, but
      they also allow you to open checking, retirement, and
      charitable-giving accounts. They have fully built-out sup-
      port teams and physical locations for enhanced customer
      support. They have stood the test of time and are likely to
      exist for decades to come.
      ii. Negatives: They can have somewhat aggressive teams of
      "advisors" that encourage you to invest in high-fee invest-
      ment products. Their websites and mobile apps can be
      confusing for new investors to navigate. They either don't
      allow you to or severely limit investing in alternative
      assets, like crypto and collectibles (as of the writing of
      this book).
   b. Mobile-first brokers (a.k.a. "investing apps")
      i. Positives: A very friendly user interface makes these apps
      easy to navigate, even for brand-new investors. Nearly
      all mobile-first brokers offer fractional share investing,
      allowing you to buy a fraction of a stock or ETF for as
      little as $1. These apps are on the cutting edge of the
      investing world, oftentimes allowing you to invest in
      alternative assets like crypto and even collectibles.
      ii. Negatives: Many do not allow you to open retirement
      or charitable accounts (as of the writing of this book).

There are no physical locations to visit. They are still relatively new, so long-term viability could be a question (though SIPC insurance will protect most, if not all, of your investments in the event of a bankruptcy).

   c. Robo advisors

      i. Positives: They provide a hands-off investment experience, usually at a fairly low price. They allow you to open retirement accounts as well as brokerage accounts. They can automatically implement advanced tax saving strategies.

     ii. Negatives: Even though the fees appear low, they can still add up over time. They give you limited investment choices. They have no physical locations.

2. Once you decide which category of broker you want to move forward with, you need to choose which specific broker you like the most. Most are very similar, and your decision will likely come down to which is the easiest to use for you. It's important to note that you can open multiple brokerage accounts and transfer your assets between them (usually tax- and fee-free) if you'd like to make a switch (see Section 2.4 on page 29 for a guide on this).

3. When you've made your choice, simply navigate to the broker's website or their app on the app store and sign up for a brokerage account. Regulatory compliance and tax laws require that brokers collect certain personal information (such as your Social Security number, address, and employment status); so, while it may feel odd to enter all this in, know that it's completely normal and your broker is obligated to protect this information.

4. Once your brokerage account is open, your broker will provide instructions on how to fund it (usually by connecting a bank account).

Recap

1. Choose where to open your brokerage account: this could be with a more established name, a newer investing app, or a hands-off robo advisor.

2. Enter the information required by the broker, such as your name, address, date of birth, and Social Security number, and wait for your account to be verified.
3. Fund your account with a transfer from your checking account.

Congrats! You've officially opened your brokerage account and are one step closer to becoming an investor. To learn how to actually *invest* the money inside your brokerage account, turn to Section 2.5 on page 32.

2.2   How to Open Roth and Traditional IRAs

Setup Time	Maintenance Time	Function
15 Minutes	N/A	Make Money

Brokerage accounts (described in Section 2.1) are nice, but they don't offer any special tax benefits. If you want to save money on taxes today, or in retirement, consider opening a Roth and/or a traditional IRA (these accounts are USA-specific). Functionally, they work very similarly to brokerage accounts in that you open them on your own (your workplace doesn't have anything to do with them) and you're responsible for both contributing money to them and investing that money.

Essential Terminology

Traditional IRA: A self-managed retirement account (IRA stands for "Individual Retirement Account") that allows you to deduct contributions from your taxable income in the year they're made, but you owe taxes on these funds when they're withdrawn in retirement. In other words, it saves you taxes TODAY in return for a tax on your earnings TOMORROW. For example, if your taxable income for the year was $50,000 and you contributed $5,000 to your traditional IRA, your taxable income would drop to $45,000. This would be $5,000 × (your tax rate, for example, 20%) = $1,000 in taxes (assuming that 20% tax rate). Also, anything that happens inside a traditional IRA that is normally taxed in a brokerage account (capital gains, dividends, interest, etc.) isn't taxed as long as these funds stay within the traditional IRA.

Roth IRA: Similar to the traditional IRA, but you save taxes *tomorrow* while paying taxes *today*. Funds you contribute to your Roth IRA don't save you any taxes in the year you contribute them, but they grow tax-free (just like the funds within a traditional IRA), and you can withdraw them completely tax-free in retirement. For example, if you contribute $5,000 to a Roth IRA every year for forty years and receive a 10% annual rate of return (this is for illustrative purposes only; investing in the real world involves risk), your balance would grow to over $2.4 million. If this was in a traditional IRA, these funds would be taxed at the same rate as your wages when you withdraw them, but because they're in a Roth IRA, this money is 100% tax-free as long as you wait until the minimum withdrawal age (described below).

Contribution Limit: Because the tax-saving benefits of both IRAs are so powerful, the amount you can contribute to them is limited. As of 2023, the maximum you can contribute (total) between a Roth and traditional IRA is $6,500 (or $7,500 if you're age 50 or older). There are also limits based on income and whether you're already covered by a retirement plan at work (in the Traditional IRA's case), so be sure to research the current limits before opening an IRA to ensure you're eligible.

Minimum Withdrawal Age: For both Roth and traditional IRAs, you must (currently, as of 2023) wait until at least age 59.5 before you withdraw funds from these accounts without incurring penalties.

Broker: It's a fancy way to refer to the company that hosts your investing accounts. Just as you associate "banks" like Chase, Wells Fargo, and Bank of America with checking accounts, you can associate "brokers" like Fidelity, Vanguard, and Charles Schwab with investing accounts. Brokers are specifically licensed to facilitate transactions on the stock market, whereas most "regular" banks aren't. Note that the brokers I discuss here are specific to the USA: each country generally has its own set of brokers, though there are some that operate in dozens, or even hundreds, of different countries. See a list of my favorite brokers, both US and non-US, at nicktalksmoney.com/investingapps.

Ingredient List

Required:

- Computer or smartphone
- Personal identification (such as a driver's license or passport)
- Social Security number or ITIN
- Proof of address (utility bill, rental agreement, etc.)

Optional:

- My list of my favorite mobile-first brokers at nicktalksmoney .com/investingapps

Recipe

1. Determine whether you're eligible to contribute to a Roth and/or traditional IRA. The IRS (the taxing authority in the USA) has a page detailing all eligibility criteria at irs.gov/retirement-plans/plan-participant-employee/retirement-topics-ira-contribution-limits.
2. Decide whether you want to contribute to a Roth IRA, traditional IRA, or a mixture of both (though you're still capped at the total annual contribution limit [$6,500 for 2023] between the two accounts).
   a. If you expect to be in a higher tax bracket in retirement (due to either rising tax rates over time or increased income), a Roth IRA may be more beneficial to you.

b. If you'd rather save tax money today, and you expect to be in a lower tax bracket in retirement, a traditional IRA may be more beneficial to you.

3. Choose a broker. The major decision here is whether you want to choose one of the older, more established brokers like Fidelity, Vanguard, or Charles Schwab, go with one of the newer, mobile-first brokers, or want the hands-off investing experience that robo advisors provide. You can find a list of my favorite brokers at nicktalksmoney.com/investingapps.

4. Once you decide which broker you want to use, submit an application to open a Roth and/or a traditional IRA. Regulatory compliance and tax laws require that brokers collect certain personal information (such as your Social Security number, address, and employment status). So, while it may feel odd to enter all this in, know that it's completely normal and your broker is obligated to protect this information.

5. Once your IRA is open, your broker will provide instructions on how to fund it (usually by connecting a bank account).

6. *The important part:* unlike a workplace retirement plan (such as a 401(k)), the money you contribute to your IRA isn't automatically invested. You need to manually invest the money after it's contributed to the account (see full instructions on how to do this in Section 2.6 on page 36).

Recap

1. Determine whether you're even eligible to contribute to an IRA (mainly based on income and if you're covered by a workplace retirement plan).

2. Decide between a Roth IRA, traditional IRA, or a mixture of the two (though the total annual contribution limit stays the same).

3. Choose a broker to host your IRA, and complete the application to open one.

4. Fund your account and *invest* this money so it isn't sitting there in cash for more than 30 years.

2.3   How to Open a 401(k)

Setup Time	Maintenance Time	Function
20–30 Minutes	10 Minutes per Month	Make Money

> Just signed up for my company's 401(k)! Though I'm a little nerv-
> ous because I've never run that far before . . .
> > —*every new hire after school failed to teach*
> > *them anything about money*

No, a 401(k) isn't a race; it's the most popular workplace-
sponsored retirement plan in the USA. If you have a full-time job
that isn't working in healthcare or for the government, chances are
your job offers a 401(k) (if you work in healthcare or the government, you'll have similar plans called 403(b)s or TSPs).

Essential Terminology

401(k): A retirement plan offered by non-government, non-
healthcare employers that allows employees to invest a portion of
their salary on a pre-tax basis. This means, much like a traditional
IRA detailed in Section 2.2, the money contributed to your 401(k) is
deducted from your taxable income the year it's contributed, but it's
taxed at the same tax rate as your ordinary income when you withdraw it in retirement. The funds within a 401(k) also grow tax-free.

401(k) Match: The amount of money your employer contributes to
your 401(k). Yeah, you heard that right: employers often incentivize their employees to contribute to their 401(k)s by "matching" the
contributions made by an employee up to a certain limit. For example, if a company matched employee contributions dollar-for-dollar
up to 5% of their total salary, an employee earning a $100,000 salary
that contributes 5% to their 401(k) would receive a total contribution of $10,000 to their 401(k): $5,000 from their own money and

$5,000 from their employer. The best part? Just like the money you contribute to your 401(k), the money your employer contributes isn't taxed until you eventually withdraw it in retirement. This is the closest thing to "free money" you'll find in the working world.

Ingredient List

Required:

- Employer that offers a 401(k)
- Personal identification (such as a driver's license or passport)
- Social Security number or ITIN
- Proof of address (utility bill, rental agreement, etc.)

Recipe

1. Ask your employer whether they offer a 401(k). If not, consider opening one of the IRAs described in Section 2.2. If so, continue.
   a. Note: many employers require that employees meet certain service and age requirements before they contribute to a 401(k). The most common example is being required to work at the company for twelve months and be at least 21 years of age. This stops seasonal or shorter-term workers from opening a 401(k), only to leave the company shortly after.
2. Enroll in your company's 401(k) plan, which is typically through an online portal.
   a. Ask your company's H.R. (human resources) department for help, if needed.
3. Decide how much you want to contribute to your 401(k). As mentioned in the terminology section, 401(k) matches are seen by many as essentially "free money," so it almost always makes sense to contribute at least up until the maximum limit of the match. Most company matches fall in the 2%–6% range. Your contributions will automatically be deducted from your paychecks and invested into the funds you choose.
   a. The amount an individual can contribute to their 401(k) is limited (the 2023 limit is $22,500), though employers can contribute additional money on top of this.

4. Choose your investments. 401(k) plans typically offer a mix of mutual funds (diversified, but higher fees), index funds (diversified, lower fees), and target date funds (diversified, automatically get less risky as you age, medium amount of fees).
   a. Section 2.5 on page 32 goes into more detail about how to choose the right investments for your situation.
5. Make your beneficiary elections. This is who receives access to your 401(k) in the event of your death. This is typically your spouse and/or kids. If you're unmarried and don't have kids, it's common to elect your parents as beneficiaries.
6. Monitor and analyze. 401(k)s are about as hands-off as it gets: once you elect your contribution percentage and choose your investments, it'll work automatically until you change something. As your income or risk tolerance changes, you can increase/decrease your contributions or change your investments, though the best practice is usually to just leave it alone.

Recap

1. Confirm that your employer offers a 401(k). If they do, enroll in it with the help of H.R. (if needed).
2. Decide on your contribution amount; pay attention to the employer match when doing so.
3. Choose investments while being wary of the higher-fee mutual funds.
4. Add beneficiaries.
5. Adjust when needed, but otherwise leave it alone.

2.4   How to Change Brokers

Setup Time	Maintenance Time	Function
20–30 Minutes	N/A	Manage Money

Few people open bank accounts with the intention of switching to another bank after a couple of years, just like few people ever plan on changing brokers. However, an event may happen where you want to change brokers (the new one has lower fees, a more intuitive interface, better service, etc.), and the process isn't as complicated as you might expect it to be. No, you don't have to sell all your stocks at your old platform (and pay taxes on the gains); you simply transfer the money to your bank account, and then move this money to your new broker. You can transfer your stocks (and most other holdings) directly from your old broker to your new broker using a process called an "account rollover" or an "asset transfer." These are commonly done with old 401(k)s after you leave a company (see Section 10.4).

Essential Terminology

Account Rollover/Asset Transfer: The act of directly transferring your assets from one broker to another, usually without needing to sell (and potentially incur taxes on) your stocks and funds. These are commonly used when transferring an old workplace 401(k) into a self-managed IRA, or when changing brokers. There may be small fees charged by the broker you're transferring your account(s) away from, but the receiving broker typically doesn't charge you anything and may even offer a reimbursement of the fees charged by the old broker to incentivize you to make the switch.

Broker: It's a fancy way to refer to the company that hosts your brokerage account. Just as you associate "banks" like Chase, Wells Fargo, and Bank of America with checking accounts, you can associate "brokers" like Fidelity, Vanguard, and Charles Schwab with brokerage accounts. Brokers are specifically licensed to facilitate transactions on the stock market, whereas most "regular" banks aren't. Note that the brokers I discuss here are specific to the USA: each country generally has its own set of brokers, though there are some that operate in dozens, or even hundreds, of different countries. See a list of my favorite brokers, both US and non-US, at nicktalksmoney.com/investingapps.

Ingredient List

Required:

- Old 401(k), brokerage account, or IRA you want to transfer to another platform
- Computer or smartphone
- An account with the broker you wish to transfer your old account(s) to

Recipe

1. Contact your new broker and inform them that you wish to transfer your old account(s) held at a different broker to their platform. They'll walk you through their specific process and provide you with the necessary forms/instructions.
2. Gather the information of your old accounts, and use it to complete the transfer of assets paperwork. You'll need to provide information for the account(s) that is being moved, such as:
   a. Institution where the account is held
   b. Account type (brokerage, IRA, 401(k), etc.)
   c. Account number
   d. The assets you wish to transfer
3. Before you submit the transfer paperwork, ensure you download the most recent statement from your old broker that lists all the account holdings. Then submit the transfer paperwork. You'll typically have to wait a few days up to a few weeks before the asset transfer is completed.
4. Confirm the transfer has been completed successfully. Compare the assets in your new account with the statement from your old broker to ensure nothing is missing and to see whether any of your funds had to be liquidated (a.k.a. sold and turned into cash) during the transfer. If they did, no worries (though you may owe taxes on the sale); just ensure you reinvest this money. If you're done using your old broker, ensure you officially close your account with them once the transfer has been completed successfully.

Recap

1. Contact your new broker and inform them that you wish to transfer the account(s) in question.
2. Complete the required transfer of assets paperwork using data from your old account(s) such as the account number and type.
3. Download the most recent statement from your old account(s), then submit the transfer paperwork.
4. Once the transfer has been completed, ensure it was successful by comparing the assets transferred with the old account statement you downloaded.
5. Close your old account if you don't intend on using that broker anymore.

2.5   How to Choose What to Invest In

Setup Time	Maintenance Time	Function
30 Minutes	N/A	Manage Money

When you're just starting out, the number of investments available to you can feel downright intimidating. Do you want to invest in the stock of your favorite car company? Would you rather spread your money out over thousands of different stocks? Do stocks feel too risky for you, and you'd rather get a fixed return instead?

This section won't have a "Recipe" section, but it will go over the five major asset types you can invest in via the stock market, the pros and cons of each, and what type of investor is typically drawn to each asset.

Pros and Cons of the Five Major Asset Types

1. Stocks

Definition: A small slice of ownership in a single company.
Pros:
- Growth Potential: If you invest in the right companies, stocks could bring you higher returns than any other asset on this list.

- Liquidity: Stocks, especially the stock of large companies, are very easy to buy and sell on the open market.

Cons:
- Higher Risk: Because you'll likely concentrate your bets around a handful of companies, you'll live and die with how well they perform.
- Time Commitment: Because you need to put significant thought and consideration behind choosing which stocks to invest in, and continue to actively manage your holdings once you invest in them, stocks require the highest time commitment of any asset on this list.

Who generally invests in stocks: new investors who don't know their other options, people who view investing as a fun game, and investors who believe they have some kind of advantage in picking stocks over everyone else (newsflash: you don't).

2. Index Funds

Definition: A "basket" of hundreds, or sometimes thousands, of stocks that you can invest in very similarly to a stock. They aim to passively track the performance of a stock market "index," like the S&P 500 (a group of 500 of the largest US-based companies) or the total stock market.

Pros:
- Diversification: Because your investment is spread across so many stocks, you aren't significantly impacted by the poor performance of a single stock.
- Passive: Because you aren't actively researching and picking individual stocks, index funds require very little time from you.
- Low Fees: Passively managed index funds have fees that can be 100× less than mutual funds, but generate equal (or often better) returns (https://mba.tuck.dartmouth.edu/bespeneckbo/default/AFA611-Eckbo%20web%20site/AFA611-S8C-FamaFrench-LuckvSkill-JF10.pdf).

Cons:
- Limited Upside: Because your holdings are so diversified, you won't ever get the moonshot returns that being an early investor in a stock like Amazon or Apple would provide you.

- Slightly Less Liquid: Index funds can only be bought and sold after the stock market has closed, so they're noticeably less liquid than stocks.

Who generally invests in index funds: those who want investing to be as passive as possible, don't like paying high fees, and are comfortable opting for a "smoother ride" than stocks provide (lower upside risk, but also lower downside risk).

3. Mutual Funds

Definition: Similar to index funds, but instead of passively tracking an index of stocks, they are controlled by professional investment managers who try to provide outsized returns.

Pros:

- Diversification: Because your investment is spread across many different stocks, you typically aren't significantly impacted by the poor performance of a single stock (unless the fund bet very heavily on it).
- Reactive: Because mutual funds are actively managed, a fund manager can take advantage of, or try to protect the fund from, market trends in real time.

Cons:

- High Fees: Professional management is expensive, so it's not uncommon for mutual funds to charge fees that are 100×+ higher than similar index funds.
- Unexpected Taxes: When mutual funds sell out of a stock they're holding, the profits can be sent as a distribution to investors. The problem? These often bring an unexpected tax bill.
- Poor Performance: The combination of high fees and human management lead nearly every mutual fund to underperform similar index funds over any significant period of time (https://mba.tuck.dartmouth.edu/bespeneckbo/default/ AFA611-Eckbo%20web%20site/AFA611-S8C-FamaFrench- LuckvSkill-JF10.pdf).

Who generally invests in mutual funds: to be frank, it's typically new investors who don't know any better. I don't know many people who would be ok with paying higher fees for lower returns. In my opinion, it appears that the main reason they still exist is because they are cash cows for the companies that offer them.

4. Exchange Traded Funds (ETFs)

Definition: ETFs are also pools of money from many investors who invest in a large basket of stocks. They can either be passively managed, like index funds, or actively managed, like mutual funds.
Pros:
- Liquidity: Their main advantage over index and mutual funds is that they are traded just like stocks; you don't need to wait until the end of the trading day to buy or sell them.

The rest of the Pros/Cons list entirely depends on whether the ETF is passively or actively managed.

Who generally invests in ETFs: people who are drawn to either index or mutual funds, but want a little more flexibility.

5. Bonds

Definition: Bonds are basically IOUs offered by governments, municipalities, or companies. When you buy a bond, you're lending money to one of these entities at a fixed interest rate over a certain period of time.
Pros:
- Less Risky: Because you're buying a piece of debt at a fixed interest rate, you know exactly how much money you'll make from the bond if you hold it until maturity. Its value isn't correlated with the stock market.
- Income Stream: While holding the bond, you'll receive a steady stream of interest payments.

Cons:
- Interest Rate Risk: Bonds can be sold on the secondary market before they expire, and, since higher-interest bonds pay the holder more, they're valued more than bonds with lower interest rates. If you buy a bond in a low-interest rate environment, and interest rates increase, your bond will be worth less on the secondary market (which only really matters if you want to sell it).

- Credit Risk: Depending on who you buy the bond from, you run the risk of them not paying you back. This is why you'll see unstable companies offering higher interest rates on the bonds they issue than the US government, for example.
- Limited Upside: Unlike stocks, you know exactly what you'll be paid from a bond right when you buy it.

Who generally invests in bonds: conservative investors and those who are approaching retirement age. Historically, stocks have averaged an annual return of around 10%, while bonds have averaged just 5% (https://www.forbes.com/advisor/investing/stocks-vs-bonds/#:~:text=Historically%2C%20stocks%20have%20higher%20returns,on%20bonds%20is%20about%205%25). However, in the short run, stocks are much more volatile than bonds, which makes bonds an attractive option for retirees who need a stable source of income from their investments to live off of.

2.6   How to Buy Your First Stock

Setup Time	Maintenance Time	Function
5 Minutes	N/A	Manage Money

Investing is too complicated.
—*someone who has never bought a stock before*

Note: This section assumes that you've already followed the instructions in Sections 2.1 or 2.2 and have an investing account open.
Investing in stocks used to be a big ordeal where you'd call up a broker, ask them what stocks they recommend buying, then give them permission to make the trade on your behalf. Now? All you have to do (once you have a brokerage account or IRA) is log into your account and tap a couple of buttons. The whole process can be completed in less than a minute once you know what you're doing.

Essential Terminology

Stock: A small slice of ownership in a company. If the company grows, the stock will likely increase in price. If the company performs poorly, the stock will likely decrease in price.

Fractional Share Investing: Allows you to invest in a piece of a stock, instead of being required to buy the full share. For example, if you had $150 and you wanted to invest that into a stock that costs $100, you could buy 1.5 shares of that stock: $100 bought you a full share and $50 bought you half of a share. Some platforms allow you to invest in fractions as small as $1.

Market Order: When buying a stock, a market order will ensure you buy a stock at its current price as soon as possible.

Ticker Symbol: A short combination of letters used as a nickname for a specific company's stock on the stock market. It's usually an abbreviation of the company's name, but it doesn't have to be. For example, Tesla's ticker symbol is TSLA, and Apple's is AAPL.

Limit Order: When buying a stock with a limit order, you set a specific price at which you're willing to buy the stock, and the order doesn't fill until the stock price reaches that number. For example, let's say you want to buy a stock that's currently priced at $110, but you think its price will fall soon; you can enter a limit order for $100. This will ensure you don't buy the stock unless its price falls to $100 or less.

Ingredient List

Required:

- Computer or smartphone
- Brokerage account and/or an IRA

Optional:

- My list of my favorite mobile-first brokers at nicktalksmoney .com/investingapps

Recipe

1. Log into your brokerage account/IRA and look for a button that says something like "Buy," "Trade," "Invest," or "Place an Order." Sometimes, you may have to search for the stock/fund you want to invest in, and the "Buy" button will appear on that page.
2. Choose what you want to invest in and enter its ticker symbol. We covered this in detail in Section 2.5, so we won't dive deeper into that here.
3. Determine how much you want to buy. Thankfully, fractional share investing makes this easy since it allows you to invest an exact dollar amount instead of having to calculate how many full shares you can afford.
4. Choose the order type. Unless you have a magic crystal ball that tells you future stock prices, it almost always makes sense to stick with a market order.
5. Some brokers will make you choose a "time in force," which is when the trade will go through. Again, for nearly every investor (especially new ones), it makes sense to leave this as "Day." This just means that your order will go through as soon as possible on the day you place the order.
6. Speaking of placing the order, it's time to place the order! Some brokers may make you preview the order, which is a great time to ensure everything looks correct. If it does, click "confirm" and *congratulations!* You're officially an investor.
7. If you want to sell a stock, the process is almost identical, but you select "sell" instead of "buy."

Recap

1. Log into the account you want to make an investment with and find the "buy" button.
2. Choose what you want to invest in and enter its ticker symbol.
3. Determine how much you want to buy.
4. Choose the order type (when in doubt, go with a market order).
5. Confirm and place your order.

   Happy investing!

2.7   How to Invest as a Kid (or for Your Kids)

Setup Time	Maintenance Time	Function
30 Minutes	N/A	Make Money

In order to open a brokerage account or IRA of your own, you need to be at least 18 years old. However, that doesn't mean that your kids can't start taking advantage of the compound interest provided by the stock market before they even know how to talk using a custodial account.

Essential Terminology

Custodial Account: A brokerage account (or Roth IRA, though the child needs legitimately earned income to contribute) held in the name of your child but managed by a parent or guardian until the child reaches the age of majority for their state (usually between ages 18 and 21), when they get full control of the account. The assets inside of a custodial account legally must be used for the child's benefit, so parents can't dip into these funds to buy themselves a jet ski.

Broker: A fancy way to refer to the company that hosts your brokerage account. Just like you associate "banks" like Chase, Wells Fargo, and Bank of America with checking accounts, you can associate "brokers" like Fidelity, Vanguard, and Charles Schwab with brokerage accounts. Brokers are specifically licensed to facilitate transactions on the stock market, whereas most "regular" banks aren't. Note that the brokers I discuss here are specific to the USA: each country generally has its own set of brokers, though there are some that operate in dozens, or even hundreds, of different countries.

Ingredient List

Required:

- Personal identification (such as a driver's license or passport) for the parent/guardian

- Social Security number or ITIN of both the child and the parent/guardian
- Personal information (such as address and date of birth, for both the child and the parent/guardian

Recipe

1. Choose a custodial account provider. Many banks and brokers offer custodial accounts, so it may be worth seeing if your current bank or broker offers them.
2. Choose an account type. If your child is earning active income from a part-time job, it may be worth considering a custodial Roth IRA. If not, you'll likely need to stick with a custodial brokerage account.
3. Submit an application to open a custodial account. You'll be required to provide information such as:
   a. The Social Security number or ITIN of both the child and the parent/guardian.
   b. Address of both parties (verification may be needed).
   c. Date of birth of both parties (verification may be needed).
4. Choose investment options. If your provider is a broker (not a bank), you'll likely have access to most, if not all, of the same investment options you'd get in a normal brokerage account.
5. Come up with a funding plan. How often is the child (if old enough to work) and/or the parent/guardian making contributions to the plan?
   a. If you plan to contribute tens of thousands of dollars to a child's plan in any given year, be mindful of gift tax limitations. If not, you don't need to worry about gift tax.
6. Remember that funds in a custodial account, if withdrawn, must legally be used for the child's benefit.
7. When the child reaches their state's age of majority (between 18 and 21, depending on the state), the parent/guardian is kicked off the account and the child assumes complete control of the account, which is now a standard brokerage account (or Roth IRA, if it was previously a custodial Roth IRA).

Recap

1. Choose a custodial account provider (large brokers tend to work best).
2. Choose either a custodial brokerage account or a custodial Roth IRA (only if the child has earned income).
3. Submit an application for an account.
4. Decide what to invest in.
5. Decide how much money you'll contribute to the account.
6. The account is passed off to the child when they reach their state's age of majority (between ages 18 and 21).

Chapter 3
Credit

3.1 How to Decide When to Use a Debit Card vs a Credit Card

Setup Time	Maintenance Time	Function
10 Minutes	N/A	Spend Money

Deciding which piece of plastic you should use to pay for your expenses can be a surprisingly controversial topic, depending on who you ask. If you ask your mom for her opinion, she might tell you to use a debit card for everything. If you ask your dad for his, he might say credit cards are the way to go. If you ask your best friend, they might say they use debit for some expenses and credit for others. So, who's right?

Essential Terminology

Debit Card: A payment card linked directly to your checking account. When you buy something with a debit card, the money is pulled directly from your checking account to make the payment. When opening a checking account with most banks, you'll automatically be sent a debit card tied to that checking account.

Credit Card: A payment card that lets you borrow money from the credit card issuer (a bank) up to a certain credit limit, but this money must be paid back in full (usually within 1.5 to 2 months) to avoid owing interest to the bank. When you buy something with a credit card, you're spending the bank's money, not your own. You need to apply for credit cards in order to receive them. Unlike debit cards, credit cards often offer reward points in the form of travel rewards or cash-back for everyday spending.

Credit Score: A number that tells the bank how trustworthy a person is when it comes to borrowing money; think of it as your financial report card. From the most-important to the least-important, it's based on your on-time credit card payments, how much of your credit you use (the lower, the better), your length of credit history, how many different types of credit you have access to (the more, the better), and whether you've recently opened up a new line of credit (this will temporarily hurt your credit score). Credit scores range from 300 on the low end to 850 being perfect: 650 to 700 is considered fair, 700 to 750 is considered good, and anything over 750 is considered excellent. Having a high credit score is important because it will give you the best interest rates (thereby saving you a significant amount of money) on things like mortgages and car loans.

Ingredient List

Required:

- Bank account
- Debit card
- Credit card

Optional:

- The list of my favorite credit cards at nicktalksmoney.com/myfavcards

Pros and Cons

Debit Cards

Pros:
- Debit cards limit overspending, as you can only spend money that is actually in your bank account.
- Don't charge interest.

- Simplicity: you don't need to keep track of multiple cards and payment due dates.

Cons:
- Limited fraud protection when compared to a credit card. If someone steals your debit card, they have direct access to your bank account until you freeze it or cancel it.
- Lack of credit building. Using a debit card doesn't help you build your credit score.
- Overdraft fees. Unlike credit cards, which will just decline the transaction if it will push you over your spending limit, debit cards often charge you an overdraft fee if you make a purchase that exceeds your available funds.

Credit Cards

Pros:
- Responsible credit card use builds your credit score.
- Advanced fraud protection. You won't be held responsible for unauthorized transactions on your credit card, and since a thief that steals your credit card information is spending the bank's money, not yours, you won't feel any short-term pain in your bank account while the fraud is sorted out.
- Rewards and benefits. As an incentive to sign up for credit cards, nearly all of them offer some sort of cash-back or travel rewards in return for everyday spending. To further encourage sign-ups, many cards also offer sign-up bonuses, potentially worth hundreds of dollars, for reaching certain spending goals within a certain period of time of signing up for your credit card. Furthermore, it's common for credit cards to come with additional perks, such as purchase protection, travel insurance, rental car insurance, fee-free spending internationally, and more.

Cons:
- Fees and interest charges. This is the big one: if you don't pay off your credit card statement in full by its due date, you'll be charged some of the highest interest rates you'll ever be subject to in your life. This can easily lead to an unmanageable debt spiral if you miss a couple of months of payments.

- Temptation to overspend. When you have a credit card with a multi-thousand-dollar spending limit, you may be tempted to spend up to that limit, even if you don't actually have that much money in your bank account.
- Your credit score has the potential to go down if you miss payments, consistently spend the majority of your credit limit, or open many different lines of credit in a short period of time.

Recipe

1. Evaluate your spending habits. Be honest with yourself: are you a disciplined-enough spender to not overspend with credit cards and make on-time payments every month? Or do you know you'd spend less money if you stuck with a debit card?
   a. If you answered yes to the first question (and were completely honest with yourself), you may benefit from using credit cards for most (if not all) of your transactions.
   b. If you answered yes to the second question but want to slowly incorporate credit card use to take advantage of the benefits they provide, continue to see other methods where you can incorporate credit card use without worrying about overspending.
2. Mostly debit method: build credit with small transactions. Put small, recurring transactions, like utility bills and streaming subscriptions, on your credit card, and pay for everything else with your debit card. As long as your credit card is on autopay, you'll build credit without ever worrying about spending above your means or accruing interest charges.
3. Credit-optimized method: use a credit card to pay for categories, like groceries or gas, that it provides the highest rewards for, and use a debit card to pay for everything else. This will maximize the benefits you receive from your credit card while limiting your credit card spending to a small handful of categories that you may be less likely to overspend on.
4. Mostly credit method: this is only for the most disciplined of the mixed debit/credit card users, but this method entails paying for every smaller expense with a credit card while paying for larger

transactions with your debit card. Putting the large transactions on your debit card has two benefits: 1) deducting that money directly from your bank account makes it feel more real, causing you to really think about large purchases before you make them, and 2) keeping these large purchases off your credit card will lower the amount of your available credit that you use, which has a positive impact on your credit score.

5. No matter how you decide to incorporate credit cards into your life, the #1 rule you *must* follow is to turn on autopay for the entire balance amount every month. This means, as long as you always have enough money in your bank account to cover these payments, you won't need to worry about interest charges.

Recap

1. Be honest with yourself: will you be someone who COSTS the credit card company money or someone who *makes* the credit card company money?
2. If you want to slowly introduce credit cards into your life to take advantage of their benefits, use one of the three methods I described: the mostly debit method, the credit-optimized method, or the mostly credit method.
3. If you use credit cards, *always turn on autopay for the full statement balance every month.* As long as you don't ever spend more money than you actually have in your bank account, this will remove most of the major potential downsides of credit card use (with the only remaining one being the potential to overspend).

3.2 How to Open Your First Credit Card

Setup Time	Maintenance Time	Function
30 Minutes	N/A	Manage Money

If you read Section 3.1, you understand why it can be a good idea for many to incorporate credit card use into their lives. They can help you build your credit score, earn rewards for everyday purchases, provide increased fraud protection, and offer perks like built-in travel insurance. However, opening one isn't quite as straightforward as opening a debit card, so let's run through the process.

Essential Terminology

Credit Card: A payment card that lets you borrow money from the credit card issuer (a bank) up to a certain credit limit, but this money must be paid back in full (usually within 1.5 to 2 months) to avoid owing interest to the bank. When you buy something with a credit card, you're spending the bank's money, not your own. You need to apply for credit cards in order to receive them. Unlike debit cards, credit cards often offer reward points in the form of travel rewards or cash-back for everyday spending.

Secured Credit Card: Beginner-friendly credit cards that require the cardholder to submit a cash deposit (usually a couple hundred dollars) as collateral. This deposit acts as a safeguard for the credit card issuer in case the cardholder doesn't pay off their credit card, which reduces risk for the company, and allows a wide range of people to be eligible to open one. This allows people with limited (or zero) credit history or poor credit scores to obtain a credit card. After a period of responsible credit card use, your deposit will be returned to you.

Credit Score: A number that tells the bank how trustworthy a person is when it comes to borrowing money; think of it like your financial report card. From most-important to least-important, it's based on your on-time credit card payments, how much of your credit you use (the lower, the better), your length of credit history, how many different types of credit you have access to (the more, the better), and whether you've recently opened up a new line of credit (this will temporarily hurt your credit score). Credit scores range from 300 on the low end to 850 being perfect: 650 to 700 is considered fair,

700 to 750 is considered good, and anything over 750 is considered excellent. Having a high credit score is important because it will give you the best interest rates (thereby saving you a significant amount of money) on things like mortgages and car loans.

Ingredient List

Required:

- Computer or smartphone
- Personal ID (driver's license or passport)
- Social Security number or ITIN
- Proof of income (pay stubs, tax returns)

Optional:

- The list of my favorite credit cards at nicktalksmoney.com/myfavcards

Recipe

1. Check your credit score by requesting a free credit report from AnnualCreditReport.com. We're assuming that your credit score will either be low or nonexistent since you're just now looking to open your first credit card.
   a. If your credit score is somehow above 580, you may qualify for a non-secured or non-student credit card. If this is the case, a wider range of cards will be available to you that you can look through at nicktalksmoney.com/myfavcards. See Section 3.3 for a more comprehensive guide on how to choose a non-secured, non-student credit card.
2. Research and compare different secured or student credit cards, as they are the most likely to accept you as a first-time credit card applicant. Most cards will be pretty similar at this level, but factors to take into account include:
   a. Deposit required (for secured cards)
   b. Rewards programs (limited at this level)

    c. Annual fees (credit cards at this level shouldn't have them)

    d. Issuing bank (if they offer higher-level cards you'll eventually be interested in, it's good to start building a relationship with them)

    e. Interest rates (also called APR—ideally, this won't matter because you'll pay off your card in full every month and never get charged interest)

3. Once you find a card that looks beginner-friendly, complete the online application. It will ask for much of the same information you'll need to provide to open a bank account, like your Social Security number, address, and date of birth, and it may even require income verification. After submitting your application, you may hear your approval decision immediately, or you may have to wait multiple days.

4. Once approved, your card will be mailed to you (again, it takes some time) and you'll need to activate it using the instructions provided along with the card before you can use it. Another thing you should do before you use the card is download the mobile app and elect for automatic monthly payments of your entire statement balance: this will greatly reduce the chance of you ever being charged interest.

5. Use one of the methods described in Section 3.1 to take full advantage of your credit card.

Recap

1. As a first-time credit card applicant, you'll likely be limited to applying for secured or student credit cards. Browse my favorites at nicktalksmoney.com/myfavcards.

2. When you find a card that suits you, complete the online application and provide the required identifying information.

3. When you receive your card, make sure you download the mobile app and elect for automatic monthly payments for the entire statement balance.

3.3   How to Open Your Next Credit Card

Setup Time	Maintenance Time	Function
30 Minutes	N/A	Manage Money

Congrats! You've used your secured/student credit card responsibly enough to build up a credit score decent enough to qualify for "real" credit cards. However, you don't want to jump on the very first credit card offer you see (which will probably be from your beginner-card issuer): this recipe will go over how to choose the best credit card available to you.

Essential Terminology

Credit Card: A payment card that lets you borrow money from the credit card issuer (a bank) up to a certain credit limit, but this money must be paid back in full (usually within 1.5 to 2 months) to avoid owing interest to the bank. When you buy something with a credit card, you're spending the bank's money, not your own. You need to apply for credit cards in order to receive them. Unlike debit cards, credit cards often offer reward points in the form of travel rewards or cash-back for everyday spending.

Secured Credit Card: Beginner-friendly credit cards that require the cardholder to submit a cash deposit (usually a couple hundred dollars) as collateral. This deposit acts as a safeguard for the credit card issuer in case the cardholder doesn't pay off their credit card, which reduces risk for the company, and allows a wide range of people to be eligible to open one. This allows people with limited (or zero) credit history or poor credit scores to obtain a credit card. After a period of responsible credit card use, your deposit will be returned to you.

Credit Score: A number that tells the bank how trustworthy a person is when it comes to borrowing money; think of it like your financial report card. From most-important to least-important, it's based on your on-time credit card payments, how much of your credit you use (the lower, the better), your length of credit history, how many different types of credit you have access to (the more, the better), and whether you've recently opened up a new line of credit (this will temporarily hurt your credit score). Credit scores range from 300 on the low end to 850 being perfect: 650 to 700 is considered fair, 700 to 750 is considered good, and anything over 750 is considered excellent. Having a high credit score is important because it will give you the best interest rates (thereby saving you a significant amount of money) on things like mortgages and car loans.

Ingredient List

Required:

- Computer or smartphone
- Personal ID (driver's license or passport)
- Social Security number or ITIN
- Proof of income (pay stubs, tax returns)

Optional:

- The list of my favorite credit cards at nicktalksmoney.com/myfavcards

Recipe

1. Check your credit score by requesting a free credit report from AnnualCreditReport.com. Credit cards will all require some level of a minimum credit score. It's important to know what yours is before you start applying for cards so you aren't hit with a wave of rejection letters (which also hurt your credit score).
2. Research and compare different credit cards (my list at nick talksmoney.com/myfavcards will help you out with this). You'll compare many of the same factors you did when you opened your first credit card:
   a. Rewards programs (for example, some cards may offer high rewards for spending at grocery stores, some for gas stations, some for travel, etc.)

b. Annual fees (cards with annual fees tend to have better rewards programs and fees; don't automatically discount them just because of the fee)
c. Issuing bank (if they offer higher-level cards you'll eventually be interested in, it's good to start building a relationship with them)
d. Interest rates (also called APR—ideally, this won't matter because you'll pay off your card in full every month and never get charged interest)

3. Once you find a card that looks like the best choice for you, complete the online application. It will ask for much of the same information you'll need to provide to open a bank account, like your Social Security number, address, and date of birth, and it may even require income verification. After submitting your application, you may hear your approval decision immediately, or you may have to wait multiple days.

4. Once approved, your card will be mailed to you (which, again, takes some time) and you'll need to activate it using the instructions mailed along with the card before you can use it. Another thing you should do before you use the card is to download the mobile app and elect for automatic monthly payments of your entire statement balance: this will greatly reduce the chance of you ever being charged interest.

5. Use one of the methods described in Section 3.1 to take full advantage of your credit card.

Recap

1. Request a free credit report from AnnualCreditReport.com to get an accurate look at your credit score, which is used to determine which cards you may qualify for.
2. When you find a card that suits you, complete the online application and provide the required identifying information.
3. When you receive your card, make sure you download the mobile app and elect for automatic monthly payments for the entire statement balance.

3.4   How to Build Your Credit Score

Setup Time	Maintenance Time	Function
30 Minutes	Conscious Action Each Month	Build Credit

One number determines everything from how much your monthly payment is on your house to whether you can apply for certain jobs: your credit score. This is why I'm such a big advocate for incorporating credit cards into your financial game plan in some way, shape, or form. This recipe will provide the ins and outs of what it takes to build an excellent credit score.

Essential Terminology

Credit Score: A number that tells the bank how trustworthy a person is when it comes to borrowing money; think of it like your financial report card. From most-important to least-important, it's based on your on-time credit card payments, how much of your credit you use (the lower, the better), your length of credit history, how many different types of credit you have access to (the more, the better), and whether you've recently opened up a new line of credit (this will temporarily hurt your credit score). Credit scores range from 300 on the low end to 850 being perfect: 650 to 700 is considered fair, 700 to 750 is considered good, and anything over 750 is considered excellent. Having a high credit score is important because it will give you the best interest rates (thereby saving you a significant amount of money) on things like mortgages and car loans.

Credit Report: A detailed report of your credit history. This is used to calculate your credit score.

Ingredient List

Required:

- Computer or smartphone
- Responsible credit habits (or a commitment to build them)

Recipe

1. Understand how your credit score is calculated. Ranked from most important to least important, the factors that impact your credit score are:

    a. Payment history (pay in full and on time and you'll be fine!)

    b. Credit utilization (aim to never have a balance equal to 30% or more of your total credit limit—the less of your credit you use, the better)

    c. Length of credit history (the credit bureaus love to see credit cards with long histories)

    d. Credit mix (having other credit lines, like student loans, mortgages, and auto loans, actually has a positive impact on your credit score)

    e. New credit applications (new credit applications will temporarily decrease your credit score, so you want to be selective with them)

2. Use AnnualCreditReport.com to request a free copy of your credit reports from all 3 major credit bureaus (the people who generate your credit reports)—Experian, TransUnion, and Equifax. These reports show where your credit currently stands, but it's also important to review them for accuracy and dispute any errors with the credit bureau.

3. If you don't have a credit card, open one (see Sections 3.2 or 3.3). It's difficult to build credit without one.

4. Paying off your credit card in full, on time is one of the best things you can do for both your credit score and your wallet (you'll avoid credit card interest). Turning on autopay for your full statement balance every month is the best way to ensure this consistently happens: even one missed payment has the potential to majorly impact your credit score.

5. Keep your credit utilization below 30%. If your total credit limit for one credit card is $1,000, you'll want to keep the balance of that card below $300. If you have two credit cards that each have a $1,000 limit (so a total combined credit limit of $2,000), you'll want to keep your total credit card balance below $600, and so on. This may seem odd, but it shows the credit bureaus that, even though you have access to a ton of credit, you don't ever come close to maxing out your card.

6. Continually monitor your credit. Many credit card apps now have credit score tracking built-in: if you see your score decrease out of nowhere, request a credit report from AnnualCreditReport .com to see what the cause is and dispute it, if necessary.

7. Maintain responsible financial habits. Living within your means, never spending more money on your credit card than you actually have in your bank account, not over-applying for credit cards, and keeping debt levels in check will go a long way in ensuring you have an excellent credit score.

   a. It's also a good idea to keep an emergency fund (see Section 1.3) on hand to avoid needing to use your credit card for large, unexpected expenses.

Recap

1. Understand that making on-time payments and keeping your credit utilization low are the two biggest determining factors of your credit score.

2. Use AnnualCreditReport.com to request a free copy of your credit reports from all 3 major credit bureaus: review and analyze them for errors.

3. Open a credit card (if you don't already have one), use it responsibly, and ensure you turn on autopay for the entire statement balance every month.

Sounds easy enough, right?

3.5   How to Build Your Kid's Credit Score Before They Can Even Walk

Setup Time	Maintenance Time	Function
45 Minutes	N/A	Build Credit

If you read Section 3.4, you know how important it is to build a good credit score. What you may *not* know is that you don't need to be 18 to start building your credit score: kids of any age can start their credit-building journey (with the help of a parent/guardian). Imagine turning 18 and instantly being eligible for the lowest interest rates on student loans, credit cards with the highest rewards, and being easily approved for any apartment/home they want to rent: that's what the gift of a good credit score can get you.

Essential Terminology

Credit Score: A number that tells the bank how trustworthy a person is when it comes to borrowing money; think of it like your financial report card. From most-important to least-important, it's based on your on-time credit card payments, how much of your credit you use (the lower, the better), your length of credit history, how many different types of credit you have access to (the more, the better), and whether you've recently opened up a new line of credit (this will temporarily hurt your credit score). Credit scores range from 300 on the low end to 850 being perfect: 650 to 700 is considered fair, 700 to 750 is considered good, and anything over 750 is considered excellent. Having a high credit score is important because it will give you the best interest rates (thereby saving you a significant amount of money) on things like mortgages and car loans.

Authorized User: An individual who is added to another person's credit card account. The authorized user will benefit from the primary cardholder's credit history and responsible credit usage (or they could suffer from poor credit usage, so be careful). Some cards have authorized user age limits (usually between 13 and 16 years old), while others don't.

Ingredient List

Required:

- Computer or smartphone
- A parent or guardian with good credit habits
- Credit card with an authorized user option (a common offering by credit cards)

Recipe

1. Research credit cards that offer the ability to add an authorized user. Factors to consider:
   a. Whether or not the card has an age limit for authorized users
   b. Whether the authorized user can receive their own card tied to the parent's/guardian's account (if this is offered by your card, it's optional)
   c. If the parent/guardian is able to set spending limits for the authorized user (the authorized user isn't required to spend anything to receive the benefits from their parent's/guardian's responsible credit use)
   d. Fees
2. Once you hone in on the right card, apply for it and add your child as an authorized user (sometimes able to be done during the application process, other times you must wait until you're approved for the card).
3. If your child DOES receive their own card tied to this account, ensure you educate them on responsible credit card use, set spending limits, and actively monitor their activity.
4. *The most important part*: The parent/guardian must do everything in their power to make on-time payments and keep credit utilization low. They're responsible not just for their own credit score, but for their child's credit score as well. If their credit score increases, so will their child's—but if their credit score decreases, so will their child's.
5. When the child turns 18, they're able to apply for their own credit cards (with what should be a fairly robust credit score), so they can be removed as an authorized user at this point.

Recap

1. Find a card that allows authorized users to be added in the child's age range.
2. Apply for the card and add the child as an authorized user.
3. The child's credit score is dependent on how the account owner manages their credit card: be responsible.

3.6 Travel Hacking: How to Use Credit Card Rewards to Travel for Free (or at a Steep Discount)

Setup Time	Maintenance Time	Function
1 Hour	2–5 Hours per Quarter	Save on Travel

Traveling these days is *expensive*. It can be hard to afford one trip per year, let alone multiple. However, as we briefly mentioned in Section 3.3, some credit cards offer reward points that can be used to help cover, or even completely pay for, common travel expenses like flights and hotels. You can earn these rewards points through everyday spending with the right credit card, but the way to rack up hundreds, if not thousands, of dollars worth of points in the shortest amount of time is by earning credit card sign-up bonuses. Dedicated travel hackers, as they're called, know this, so they open 2 to 4 credit cards per year that offer the most lucrative sign-up bonuses. This recipe will explain how to leverage credit card rewards to unlock deeply discounted travel opportunities.

Warning: Since this is dealing with spending on multiple credit cards, you should only attempt travel hacking if you are extremely organized and mindful of your spending. If you aren't, this could be a great way to get yourself into a mountain of credit card debt.

Essential Terminology

Credit Card Rewards: Many credit cards offer rewards programs that allow cardholders to earn rewards points based on their spending. Depending on your credit card, you may be able to redeem these points for flights, hotels, car rentals, cash-back, and more.

Travel Hacker: Someone who leverages credit card rewards to travel for free or at significantly discounted rates, allowing them to explore the world more affordably. They are extremely organized individuals who can easily handle having multiple credit cards open at once.

Credit Card Sign-up Bonus: Promotional offers from credit card issuers to incentivize new customers to apply for their cards. These bonuses typically come in the form of rewards points and must be earned by spending a certain amount of money on the credit card within a certain time frame of receiving it (example: spending $4,000 in your first three months with the card). Be aware that these credit card issuers offer these sign-up bonuses because they make money from the majority of people who hold their credit cards through interest paid on late payments: don't be someone who makes the credit card company money.

Transferable Points: Some credit cards have reward points that can be transferred to various airline and hotel partners, which can increase the value of these points when booking with these transfer partners.

Credit Card: A payment card that lets you borrow money from the credit card issuer (a bank) up to a certain credit limit, but this money must be paid back in full (usually within 1.5 to 2 months) to avoid owing interest to the bank. When you buy something with a credit card, you're spending the bank's money, not your own. You need to apply for credit cards in order to receive them. Unlike debit cards, credit cards often offer reward points in the form of travel rewards or cash-back for everyday spending.

Credit Score: A number that tells the bank how trustworthy a person is when it comes to borrowing money; think of it like your financial report card. Credit scores range from 300 on the low end to 850 being perfect: 650 to 700 is considered fair, 700 to 750 is considered good, and anything over 750 is considered excellent.

Ingredient List

Required:

- Computer or smartphone
- Good credit score
- Time to research and understand travel hacking

Optional:

- My curated list of credit cards with the best available sign-up bonuses and rewards programs: nicktalksmoney.com/myfavcards
- An app to track all your credit cards and sign-up bonuses: nick talksmoney.com/travelhacker

Recipe

1. Determine whether you'd be a good travel hacker. Are you extremely organized? Have you always paid your credit cards off (fully) on time? Do you have a good credit score? If you answered "yes" to all three questions, you'll probably thrive as a travel hacker. If not, it may be a little too risky for you to pursue.
2. Before you start your travel hacking journey, come up with a system to manage your credit cards and track your sign-up bonuses. Spreadsheets are a popular option here, though I prefer the free travel hacking app that you can find at nicktalksmoney.com/ travelhacker.
3. Research and find your first "travel hacking" card. Compare cards based on sign-up bonuses, spending rewards, transfer partners, credit score required, and annual fees. Warning: most good travel hacking cards do come with annual fees, though they tend to be far outweighed by the value you receive from the signing bonus.
   a. You can look through my (constantly updated) list of the top travel hacking cards here: nicktalksmoney.com/myfavcards
4. Apply for your top credit card. Only apply for one card at a time, as it could be very difficult to meet the sign-up bonus requirements for multiple cards at once (not to mention the negative hit your credit score would take from multiple applications).
5. Meet the spending requirement of your sign-up bonus. I like to do this by putting as much of my (and my girlfriend's) everyday spending on my card as possible. I also tend to apply for new cards before I make large purchases, like vacations (booked without points), car repairs, or buying new ski gear, which

makes it a lot easier to hit the sign-up bonus. If you're going to make these large purchases anyway, you might as well earn points from them (assuming you'll have no problem fully paying off your credit card)! However, you must avoid frivolous spending just for the sake of meeting a sign-up bonus. The amount of this wasted money could outweigh the benefits of your sign-up bonus.

6. The fun part: use your rewards for travel. Many credit card issuers offer travel portals where you can directly redeem your points for airfare and hotels, or you can try to find a better deal through a transfer partner (which is a bit more difficult before you know what you're doing but can stretch the value of your points much further).

7. Maximize the other benefits provided by your credit card. The best travel credit cards often offer a myriad of perks outside of their reward points. These can include airport lounge access, travel insurance, statement credits for travel expenses, or status with hotels and airlines. Utilize as many as possible to get the most value from your credit card.

8. Accumulate more points by repeating this process. In order to avoid adverse consequences to your credit score, it's recommended that you wait at least three months between getting new credit cards. So, you could potentially earn sign-up bonuses for three or four cards each year, which can amount to thousands of dollars in free travel.

9. Decide which cards to keep open. Since most of the credit cards that work best for travel hacking come with annual fees, you may decide that you don't want to keep them open for longer than you have to. However, instead of closing these cards and potentially damaging your credit score (see Section 3.4), call your credit card company using the phone number on the back of your card and ask if your card has a "downgrade" option. If so, your high annual fee card is replaced with a low or no-fee card, and your credit history stays intact.

   a. Before asking for a downgrade option or closing your cards, confirm that taking either action won't disqualify you from using your rewards points from the card you're downgrading or closing.

10. Be someone who costs the credit card companies money, not someone who makes them money. All the benefits of travel hacking are quickly erased if you start accumulating credit card debt. The interest charged on this debt will dwarf the travel benefits you receive.

Recap

1. Be honest with yourself: are you someone who's organized enough to benefit from travel hacking? Or will you just end up owing the credit card companies money?
2. Come up with a system to manage your credit cards and sign-up bonuses. My favorite free tracking app can be found here: nicktalksmoney.com/travelhacker.
3. Research and find your first travel hacking card. I keep an updated list of the top cards available here: nicktalksmoney .com/myfavcards.
4. Apply for your top credit card, and *only* your top credit card. You don't want to be approved for more than one credit at once, as it would be very difficult to hit multiple sign-up bonuses in the designated time frame.
5. Meet the spending requirements of your sign-up bonus. Offer to pay for group dinners and have everyone pay you back afterward, time your credit card application so it's right before you plan to make a large purchase, and put as many of your everyday expenses on there as possible.
6. Redeem your rewards points for free (or discounted) travel. If available, it's generally easiest to book through your credit card's travel portal, though you may find better deals by transferring these points directly to a transfer partner like an airline or hotel.
7. Ensure you take advantage of all the other benefits provided by your credit card, like travel insurance and airport lounge access.
8. Repeat this process to accumulate more rewards, but ensure you wait at least 3 months between applying for a new credit card.
9. Explore downgrading your high annual fee cards that you don't see yourself using in the future.
10. Be someone who costs the credit card companies money, not someone who makes them money.

Chapter 4
Debt

4.1 How to Differentiate Between "Good" and "Bad" Debt

Setup Time	Maintenance Time	Function
20 Minutes	N/A	Manage Money

> All debt is bad! Pull yourself up by your bootstraps and pay for everything in cash!
>
> *—your grandparents, probably*

While your grandparents' wisdom comes from the right place—debt can often be risky and unnecessary—there are many situations where debt can actually be a *good* thing. Instead of a recipe, we'll go over common types of good and bad debt.

Essential Terminology

Debt: Money that you borrow (usually from a bank) and promise to pay back at a later date. Not only will you pay back the original amount you borrowed, but you'll also pay interest on top of it (this is what incentivizes banks to give you a loan in the first place).

Good Debt: Money that you borrow that has the potential to provide long-term benefits or increase your net worth. Good debt tends to come with lower interest rates (meaning you'll be charged less for borrowing it) than bad debt.

Bad Debt: Money that you borrow that doesn't provide long-term value or improve your finances. Even worse, it tends to be used to buy liabilities (items whose value decreases over time and/or takes additional money out of your pocket with upkeep and maintenance). Bad debt tends to have higher interest rates than good debt.

Good Debt Examples

- **Federal Student Loans**: I'll start with the caveat that this entirely depends on how well you take advantage of your education. However, on average, the average college graduate makes $1.2 million more than the average high school graduate over their lifetimes (https://www.aplu.org/our-work/4-policy-and-advocacy/publicuvalues/employment-earnings/#:~:text=College%20graduates%20are%20half%20as,million%20more%20over%20their%20lifetime), so taking out low-interest student loans to attend college is an overall good financial decision. To ensure this is the case: Be intentional with your field of study, aggressively pursue internships, and make as many ambitious friends as possible while you're in school.
- **Investing in Assets**: There is risk involved, but also a significant upside potential to taking out loans to invest in rental of real estate or to buy a business. Both have the potential to increase in value over time while providing enough cash flow to cover the loan payments.

Bad Debt Examples

- **Consumer Debt**: If you want to be financially healthy, avoid consumer debt like the plague: It includes credit card debt and personal loans. These come with some of the highest interest rates you'll ever be charged, and, in all likelihood, the items you buy with them won't do anything to improve your finances.

- **Auto Loans**: Before you get too mad—I know it's essential for nearly every adult to own a car (unless you live somewhere like New York City). However, this doesn't mean that you should subject yourself to a crippling auto loan because you want to drive the fanciest car in the neighborhood. Cars are the definition of a liability: New cars lose an average of 9–11% of their value the moment you drive them off the lot (https://www .ramseysolutions.com/saving/car-depreciation#:~:text=the%20 dotted%20line.-,A%20brand%2Dnew%20car%20loses%20some where%20between%209%E2%80%9311%25,you%20drive%20 off%20the%20lot), you'll spend hundreds (or even thousands) of dollars per year on insurance, and you'll spend a similar amount on repairs and maintenance. This is all being spent on something that <u>sits unused for</u> roughly twenty-two hours per day (and that's if you're *really* getting some use out of it). Don't buy more car than you can afford (see Section 5.1 to learn how to *not* get scr*wed when buying a car).

- **Private Student Loans**: While used for a similar purpose as federal student loans, private student loans are *much* more dangerous because they come with significantly higher interest rates. When going to college, if you need loans, do everything you can to stick with lower-interest federal student loans (work, apply for scholarships and grants, etc.). If you absolutely need to take out private student loans, pay them off as soon as possible after graduating.

Recap

1. Good debt, which is (generally) lower-interest debt that has a chance to improve your financial position, can often be a smart thing to utilize.
2. Bad debt, on the other hand, comes with high interest rates and little/no chance of improving your finances. It should be avoided at all costs.

4.2   The Debt Snowball Method: The Best Way (Behaviorally) to Pay Off Debt

Setup Time	Maintenance Time	Function
20 Minutes	15 Minutes per Month	Debt Payoff

If you find yourself drowning in debt, there are two methods financial planners recommend using to escape from it: the debt snowball method (covered in this recipe) and the debt avalanche method (covered in Section 4.3). The debt snowball method focuses on the behavioral aspects of debt repayment by putting your full focus on paying off your smallest debt balances first, and then working up the ladder until you finally pay off your largest debt balance. This quickly creates a sense of accomplishment and provides motivation because you see instant progress, though the progress will slow down as you reach higher balances. However, because the snowball method purely focuses on debt balances, not interest rates, it may not be the most financially wise way to pay off your debt.

Essential Terminology

Debt: Money that you borrow (usually from a bank) and promise to pay back at a later date. Not only will you pay back the original amount you borrowed, but you'll also pay interest on top of it (this is what incentivizes banks to give you a loan in the first place).

Debt Snowball Method: A debt payoff method that focuses on creating a sense of accomplishment and providing motivation immediately by targeting your smallest debt balances (by dollar amount) first, and working your way up the ladder until you finally pay off your largest debt balance. This extra motivation is thought to make consumers more likely to pay off all of their debt, though they'll accrue more interest charges than they would if they followed the debt avalanche method (described in Section 4.3).

Interest: How much you're charged for holding your debt. For example, if you have a debt balance of $1,000 at a 10% interest rate (compounded yearly), and you don't add or subtract anything from that debt for one year, you would be charged $100 in interest and your total debt balance would rise to $1,100. Interest for the next year would be $10\% \times \$1,100 = \$110$. The longer you hold your debt, the more interest you're charged.

Ingredient List

Required:

- A list of all your debts and their balances

Optional:

- Budgeting apps (my favorites are listed at nicktalksmoney.com/budgetapps)
- A Budgeting spreadsheet (mine is available at nicktalksmoney.com/budget)

Recipe

1. List all of your debts from the smallest balance (the dollar amount of the debt) to the highest, and include what the minimum payment is on each debt. Debts could include unpaid credit cards, personal loans, auto loans, etc.
2. Create a monthly budget, including all of the minimum payments, and determine how much leftover money you have each month that can be used to make additional debt payments.
   a. Be ruthless in cutting/reducing nonessential spending.
      You're in a hole of debt: If you don't dig yourself out quickly, your finances may never fully recover.
3. Use the additional money you set aside in your budget to make an extra payment toward the smallest debt (by dollar amount) on your list.

4. Repeat until the smallest debt is paid off, and then allocate these additional funds (plus the extra money from the minimum payment you no longer owe) to paying off the next-smallest debt on your list.

5. Repeat and build your snowball. As more pieces of debt are taken care of, you'll continue to get additional funds (the former minimum payments) to put toward the next piece of debt.

6. Celebrate each piece of debt you pay off. This will help keep you focused and ensure your final goal is achieved: your final (and largest) debt balance paid off.

7. Your work isn't over once your final debt balance is paid off: You need to be intentional about building an emergency fund (Section 1.3), budgeting (Section 1.4), and investing (Chapter 2) so you don't end up in this situation again.

Recap

1. List all of your debt balances, from the smallest to the largest amount.

2. Build a budget to identify how much extra money you can allocate toward additional debt payments each month.

3. Throw all of this extra money at your smallest piece of debt. Once that is paid off, use it (plus the extra money from the minimum payment you no longer need to make) to pay off your next smallest piece of debt. Rinse and repeat, and continue to "snowball" these larger payments into the next smallest amount of debt until all of your debt is paid off.

4. Get your finances in order so this never happens again. Know what could *potentially* help with that? This book.

Tip: Before implementing an aggressive debt payoff strategy, like the debt snowball method, it's wise to build an emergency fund with three to six months' worth of expenses (see Section 1.3). This ensures your payoff plans aren't derailed if a large, unexpected expense pops up.

4.3   The Debt Avalanche Method: The Best Way (Logically) to Pay Off Debt

Setup Time	Maintenance Time	Function
20 Minutes	15 Minutes per Month	Debt Payoff

When I decide how to pay off my own debt, I immediately default to the Debt Avalanche method. Why? Because it saves me the most money. A follower of the Debt Avalanche strategy makes minimum monthly payments on each of their sources of debt and devotes any extra money they have toward paying down their highest-interest debt. Once their highest-interest debt is paid off, they focus their extra money on paying down their next highest-interest debt, and so on until all debts are paid off.

Essential Terminology

Debt: Money that you borrow (usually from a bank) and promise to pay back at a later date. Not only will you pay back the original amount you borrowed, but you'll also pay interest on top of it (this is what incentivizes banks to give you a loan in the first place).

Debt Avalanche Method: A debt payoff strategy that focuses on paying off the highest-interest debts first. By taking care of the debts with the most expensive interest rates right away, you'll save more money on interest (compared to the debt snowball method described in Section 4.2) and pay off your debt faster. However, debts with high interest rates are likely to have higher balances, so these balances may take a good amount of time to pay off. Even though paying off a $5,000 credit card balance that comes with a 20% interest rate sooner than a $1,000 loan with a 5% interest rate is the best thing to do logically, you could lose motivation due to a perceived lack of progress because it might take over a year to fully pay off the credit card.

Interest: How much you're charged for holding your debt. For example, if you have a debt balance of $1,000 at a 10% interest rate (compounded yearly), and you don't add or subtract anything from that debt for one year, you would be charged $100 in interest and your total debt balance would rise to $1,100. Interest for the next year would be 10% × $1,100 = $110. The longer you hold your debt, the more interest you're charged.

Ingredient List

Required:

- A list of all your debts and their balances

Optional:

- Budgeting apps (my favorites are listed at nicktalksmoney.com/budgetapps)
- Budgeting spreadsheet

Recipe

1. List all of your debts, their balances, their minimum payments, and their interest rates. Sort them from the highest to the lowest interest rates. If you have trouble identifying your interest rates, contact the customer support team on the platform where your loans are held. An example of how to list your debts:
   a. Credit card debt, $8,000 balance, $25 minimum payment, 20% interest rate
   b. Private student loan, $20,000 balance, $300 minimum payment, 8% interest rate
   c. Car loan, $4,000 balance, $200 minimum payment, 4% interest rate
2. Create a monthly budget, including all of the minimum payments, and determine how much leftover money you have each month that can be used to make additional debt payments.

a. Be ruthless in cutting/reducing nonessential spending.
   You're in a hole of debt: if you don't dig yourself out quickly,
   your finances may never fully recover.
3. Use the additional money you set aside in your budget to make
   an extra payment toward the highest-interest debt on your
   list.
4. Once your highest-interest debt is paid off (the credit card
   debt in our example above), focus this extra money on paying down your next highest piece of debt (the private student
   loan in the example above). Rinse and repeat until all debt
   is paid off.
5. Your work isn't over once your final debt balance is paid off:
   you need to be intentional about building an emergency fund
   (Section 1.3), budgeting (Section 1.4), and investing (Chapter 2)
   so you don't end up in this situation again.

Recap

1. List all of your debt balances, from the highest to the lowest
   interest rate.
2. Build a budget to identify how much extra money you can allocate toward additional debt payments each month.
3. Throw all of this extra money at your highest-interest piece of
   debt. Once that is paid off, use it (plus the extra money from the
   minimum payment you no longer need to make) to pay off your
   next highest-interest piece of debt. Rinse and repeat until all of
   your debt is paid off.
4. Get your finances in order so this never happens again. Know
   what could *potentially* help with that? This book.

*Tip: Before implementing an aggressive debt payoff strategy, like
the Debt Avalanche method, it's wise to build an emergency fund
with three to six months' worth of expenses (see Section 1.3). This
ensures your payoff plans aren't derailed if a large, unexpected
expense pops up.*

4.4 How to Lower Your Interest Rate by Consolidating Debt

Setup Time	Maintenance Time	Function
1 Hour	30 Minutes per Month	Debt Payoff

Another option outside of the debt snowball (Section 4.2) and debt avalanche (4.3) methods is consolidating all your debt into one, lower-interest debt balance. Consolidation is when you combine multiple debts into a single loan with (what should be, at least) a lower interest rate than the debt you previously held. This simplifies your debt payoff process since you only have to make one payment each month, and it'll save you money on interest payments (when done correctly).

Essential Terminology

Debt: Money that you borrow (usually from a bank) and promise to pay back at a later date. Not only will you pay back the original amount you borrowed, but you'll also pay interest on top of it (this is what incentivizes banks to give you a loan in the first place).
Debt Consolidation: The process of combining multiple debts into a single loan. This service is offered by most major loan providers.

Ingredient List

Required:

- A list of all your debts, their balances, and their interest rates

Recipe

1. List all of your debts: ensure you highlight their balances, interest rates, and repayment terms. This will help you evaluate whether the debt consolidation offers you find are worth it.

2. Research debt consolidation loans. You'll find dozens of financial institutions offering them, so judge them based on the following criteria:

   a. **Interest rate**: If your new loan's interest rate isn't lower than the average interest rate on your current loans, it probably won't make sense to consolidate using that loan.

   b. **Loan amount**: Debt consolidation providers have minimum and maximum loan amounts; ensure your debt balance fits within this range.

   c. **Required credit score**: Some debt consolidation loans require a higher credit score in order to qualify for them, and some don't. Beware that loans with lower credit requirements typically have higher origination fees. Speaking of which . . .

   d. **Origination fee**: This is an upfront fee charged by your debt consolidation provider to cover the cost of processing and funding the loan. It's typically a percentage of the loan amount (2% to 10%, for example, though the actual range varies) and is added to the loan, so you pay it off over time. If you have a higher credit score, you may not have to pay origination fees, but most debt consolidation loans charge them.

   e. **Repayment terms**: This is how long you have to pay the loan back. This, along with your interest rate, origination fee, and loan amount, determine what your monthly payment will be. The shorter the repayment window, the higher your monthly payment will be.

3. Calculate how much your current debt will cost you at your current payoff rate (online calculators make this easy), then see if any of the debt consolidation loans you found would save you more money, even after factoring in the origination fee.

4. If you find a debt consolidation loan that will save you money, complete the application. You'll likely have to provide identification, details of your existing debts, and proof of income.

5. Once your debt consolidation loan has been approved, use it to pay off all your existing debts in full. Then, ensure you follow the repayment terms and avoid accumulating more debt in the meantime.

Recap

1. Calculate how much your current debts will cost you to repay at your current rate of repayment.
2. Research debt consolidation options (mainly their interest rate, origination fees, and repayment terms), to see if they would save you money vs continuing your current debt payoff plan.
3. If you find a debt consolidation loan that works for your situation, apply for it. When received, use it to pay off your existing debts, and follow the repayment terms on the consolidation loan.

4.5   How to Qualify for a Debt Management Plan

Setup Time	Maintenance Time	Function
1 Hour	N/A	Debt Payoff

If you find yourself staring down a seemingly insurmountable amount of debt, you may want to consider reaching out to the National Foundation for Credit Counseling (NFCC—a nonprofit specializing in debt relief) and requesting a Debt Management Plan (DMP). A DMP can help reduce your debt, lower your interest rates with creditors, and put a structured repayment plan in place.

Essential Terminology

National Foundation for Credit Counseling (NFCC): A nonprofit institution with the goal of helping every American in need overcome their financial struggles. They have a network of 1,215 certified credit counselors willing and able to offer you help at little-to-no cost (https://www.nfcc.org/).
Debt Management Plan (DMP): A program offered by credit counseling agencies that helps individuals repay their debts.

Ingredient List

Required:

- Computer or smartphone
- Personal ID (driver's license or passport)
- A list of all your financial accounts (including debt)
- A list of the contact information of all of your creditors (who you owe debt to)

Recipe

1. Go to www.nfcc.org/ and either call them or click the action button to connect with a counselor and ask about their DMP.
2. The counselor will schedule a session with you, in which they will review your entire financial situation, ask about your goals, and analyze your debts. If they think a DMP would be helpful for your situation, they will start discussing that here.
3. If the DMP is put in place, your credit counselor will attempt to lower the interest rates on your debt and waive late fees, among other actions.
4. Once enrolled in the DMP, you will make a single monthly payment to the credit counseling agency. The agency then distributes these funds to your different creditors according to your repayment plan.
5. If all goes according to plan, your DMP will eventually lead you to becoming debt free! Since you've also been working with a credit counselor, you've also likely built up some good financial habits along the way that will decrease your chances of ending up in this much debt ever again.

Recap

1. Reach out to a credit counselor at www.nfcc.org/ (or another nonprofit credit counseling agency).

2. Provide your financial information to the credit counselor during a meeting and ask if a DMP would be beneficial for you.
3. If so, enroll in a DMP with a mutually agreed-upon repayment plan and make your monthly debt payments to your credit counseling agency for them to disburse.
4. Stick to the payment plan and eventually become debt free!

Chapter 5
Big Purchases

5.1 How to Not Get Scr*wed When Buying a Car

Setup Time	Maintenance Time	Function
1–5 Hours	N/A	Save Money

Buying a car can be an exciting experience until you realize you need to actually visit a dealership and try to get the best out of a car salesman who is an expert at getting customers to spend more money than they originally planned to. Even if you buy a car in a nontraditional method, like buying it online, there are still a few steps you need to follow to ensure your new car doesn't become an anchor that drags your net worth (Section 1.5) down to the depths of the ocean.

Essential Terminology

20/4/10 Rule: A car-buying rule of thumb recommended by financial planners to avoid overspending. It says that you should put a 20% down payment, have a loan term no longer than four years, and spend 10% or less of your take-home pay on your car (total expenses, not just the loan). If you can't make the numbers on a car work under the 20/4/10 rule, you shouldn't buy the car.

Ingredient List

Required:

- Patience
- Willingness to conduct research beforehand

Optional:

- A good credit score (see Section 3.4)

Recipe

1. Before you even think about visiting a dealership or ordering a car online, do extensive research about the kind of vehicle you want to buy. Know exactly what make and model you want to buy, and have a strong reason for wanting to buy it (otherwise you run the risk of being upsold). This familiarity will also help you when it comes to negotiations: if you know exactly what the market value of the car is, you know what your spending limit is.
2. To confirm this is the exact make and model of car that you want to buy, make sure it passes the 20/4/10 rule. Ensure you include miscellaneous expenses like insurance, fuel, and expected maintenance in the 10% calculation for the cost of your car, along with your monthly payment. Also, ensure you have enough cash saved up for the 20% down payment.
3. Get preapproved for financing from a local credit union. Credit unions typically offer the best rates on loans, and getting approved for a loan beforehand ensures 1) you don't get roped into financing at the dealership (where you'll see higher interest rates and more unfavorable terms), and 2) you know precisely what your budget is before stepping onto the lot at the dealership.
   a. It's vital that you stick to the four-year loan term described in the "20/4/10" rule. When applying for auto loans, it's common for the loan provider to ask what your maximum "monthly payment" is. They'll then stretch out a loan long enough to ensure nearly any car will fit in your budget.

4. Don't be afraid to shop around. If there are multiple dealerships in your area carrying the car you want to buy, make them compete against each other for the sale. This will get you the best price possible. You don't need to be a shrewd negotiator to do this: just mention that you're also looking at the same car down the street and mention the deal the other dealerships are offering you.

5. Intimately know the car you're buying before you buy it. Test drive it, obtain a vehicle history report (if used), and request a pre-purchase inspection (if buying from a private seller).

6. Immediately disengage with a salesperson attempting to use high-pressure tactics on you. If they say anything along the lines of "I'll need you to make a decision today; a lot of people have been looking at this car," they're probably telling what I'd call an "un-truth" that's designed to get you to make an impulsive purchase decision.

7. Once you've agreed to a deal in principle with a dealership, thoroughly review the sales contract and understand all applicable fees, the purchase price, and warranties.

   a. A note about extended warranties: According to consumer reports.org, extended warranties are viewed as "overpriced," and the main reason salespeople push them is "because they make a bundle on them in commissions" (https://www .consumerreports.org/cars/car-repair/get-an-extended-warranty-for-your-car-a1570471227/). Ultimately, deciding whether or not to purchase an extended warranty is a decision you have to make yourself. Many don't realize this, but the price of an extended warranty can be negotiated. So, if you want the extra peace of mind but don't want to feel like you're being ripped off, it doesn't hurt to try to haggle a little bit.

8. If the contract looks good, go ahead and sign it! Just be aware of the unexpected fees that come with buying a car, such as:

   a. Sales tax (can be anywhere from 0% to 8.25% of the purchase price of the car, depending on your state)

   b. Registration fees

   c. Title and license fees

   d. Insurance costs

Recap

1. Know the ins and outs of the exact make and model of the car you want to buy before you go to the dealership.
2. Budget your purchase with the 20/4/10 rule.
3. Secure preapproved auto loan financing from a local credit union.
4. Shop around at different dealerships/websites to find the best deal and pit the dealerships against each other.
5. Request a detailed vehicle history report on the car you want to buy.
6. Ignore high-pressure sales tactics.
7. Thoroughly review the sales contract and understand all applicable (and unexpected) fees.

5.2   How to Decide Between Leasing and Buying a Car

Setup Time	Maintenance Time	Function
30–60 Minutes	N/A	Manage Money

If you read Section 5.1, you now know how to buy a car without getting scr*wed. However, *buying* isn't your only option when it comes to getting a vehicle; you can also choose to *lease*. The lease vs buy debate is a big one, so this recipe will weigh the pros and cons of each.

Essential Terminology

Leasing: A car lease is when you make an agreement with a leasing company to rent a vehicle from them for a set period of time, usually two to four years. You make monthly lease payments and return the vehicle at the end of the lease term (unless you decide to buy it out).

Buying: Purchasing a vehicle, either in cash or by financing it with an auto loan. In the latter option, you'll make monthly payments on the loan until your loan is paid off and you own the car outright.

Down Payment: The initial cash lump sum you need to pay when buying a car. "Standard" down payments equal 20% of a car's purchase price.

Depreciation: When something, like a car, loses value over time. Cars depreciate due to factors like wear and tear, a decrease in reliability as the car gets older, and the availability of newer, better cars on the market.

Ingredient List

Required:

- The want/need to acquire a new vehicle
- The funds required to obtain that vehicle

Pros and Cons of Buying a Car

Pros:

- The obvious one—ownership. If you buy a car in cash, it's 100% yours and you don't need to make monthly payments on it. If you buy a car with a loan, the car becomes 100% yours after it's paid off. If you own a dependable car outright, it's possible to go *years* without making monthly car payments.
- No restrictions. Leased vehicles come with mileage limits and customization restrictions. If you buy a car, it's yours. You could paint it puke green and throw a spoiler on it if you want to.
- Resale value. Though cars tend to depreciate in value over time, there is still a healthy market for reliable used cars. At the very least, you could sell your car for parts if you wanted to change vehicles.

Cons:

- Higher upfront costs. The standard down payment when buying a car is 20% of the car's purchase price. If you're buying a $20,000 car, this means you need to have a $4,000 lump sum saved up for the down payment, plus the amount needed to cover taxes and fees.
- Depreciation. Though your car will almost certainly always hold *some* value, it will still decrease in value over time. According to Kelley Blue Book, brand-new cars lose "about 20% or more of their original value" in their first year, with cars losing an average of "60% of their original purchase price within the first five years" (https://www.kbb.com/car-advice/how-to-beat-car-depreciation/). It would be hard to justify investing in a stock that you knew was almost guaranteed to lose half of its value in the next half decade, though obviously, cars provide additional utility other than making you money. If you finance your car, and your vehicle depreciates quickly enough, you may even find yourself owning "negative equity" in the car: meaning you owe more on your loan than your car is worth.
- You cover all the maintenance and repairs. As the owner of your car, you're responsible for keeping it up and running it. This often means expensive trips to the mechanic, especially as your car gets older.

Pros and Cons of Leasing a Car

Pros:

- Lower monthly payments. Lease payments are typically lower than loan payments, which could let you drive a nicer car vs buying on the same budget.
- Warranty coverage. Typical leases include full warranty coverage, which means that you don't need to worry about paying for expensive repairs or maintenance.
- Flexibility. At the end of a lease term, you can choose to return the vehicle and lease a new one, purchase the leased car (if a

buyout option is available), or simply walk away without going through the hassle of selling a vehicle. This means you could always switch to a newer car every couple of years, and if one comes along that you really enjoy, you could opt to buy it.

Cons:

- No ownership equity. The only thing your monthly payments do is give you the right to drive the car; they don't go toward paying off a loan so you can eventually own the car.
- Continuous payments. Speaking of monthly payments, as long as you're leasing a car, you will have monthly payments. This is money that could otherwise be used for saving, investing, or other expenses.
- Mileage restrictions and additional charges. To constrain how much value a car will lose while it's leased, lease agreements typically come with mileage restrictions and additional charges if it's deemed your vehicle underwent excessive wear and tear.

5.3   How to Ensure Your Wedding Doesn't Set You Back Years Financially

Setup Time	Maintenance Time	Function
Planning a Wedding Takes a *Long* Time	N/A	Save Money

You're about to start a new chapter with the love of your life. What better way to celebrate than by blowing all of your savings on a massive party? I'm kidding, but there is some truth in there. According to popular wedding website hosting platform The Knot, the average cost of a wedding in 2022 was a whopping $30,000 (https://www.theknot.com/content/average-wedding-cost). Your wedding day can be one of the most memorable days of your life, and *every* vendor in the wedding industry knows this means you're willing to pony up some extra cash for this special occasion. This recipe will detail nine ways you can save money on your big day.

Ingredient List

- A spouse

Recipe

1. Hire professional help. It may seem counterintuitive to hire a wedding planner if you're trying to save money, but they'll know exactly where to cut costs without affecting the quality of your experience.
2. Open new credit cards with high sign-up bonuses to pay for your wedding expenses (see Section 3.6). These signup bonuses are paid to you in points that can often be redeemed for flights and hotels: Why not let your wedding expenses pay for your honeymoon?
3. Say goodbye to Saturday weddings. Since Saturdays are the most popular day for weddings by far, everything from vendors to your venue will effectively charge surge pricing. Consider opting for a Friday or Sunday wedding instead, though this may complicate the travel plans of your guests a little more than a Saturday wedding would.
4. Bring on the buffet. Buffets require less wait staff than a formal, plated dinner, which can meaningfully reduce your food cost.
5. Draw back on the drinks. If you're insistent on offering some form of cocktails, limit the selection to only a few choices. Otherwise, sticking with good old wine and beer will be the cheapest path for you.
6. Opt for a venue that doesn't need much decorating. An outdoor wedding at the beach, in the mountains, or in a nice meadow only requires a fraction of the decor of a traditional wedding venue.
7. Opt for an untraditional photo and video experience. Designate one of your trusted friends or family members as the "photographer," and have them take pictures and videos of the night

exclusively with their phone. With phone camera technology where it is right now, the quality won't be that much worse than a professional camera, and the phone pictures/videos will be much easier to share on social media! Plus, instead of needing to wait for weeks after your wedding to receive pictures from a photographer, your friend can send you the pictures that night.

8. Get the most bang for your buck by scheduling a wedding in the "off-season." Weddings slow down from November to March in most parts of the USA, so it'll be cheaper to book vendors and venues during this period than if you tried to have your wedding in prime time.

9. Does planning a wedding sound too expensive and/or stress-ful? Elope instead! This is when you marry in a simple, low-key setting with only your closest friends and family in attendance (you know, the people you'd spend the most time at your wedding with anyway). Simple elopements can cost less than $100 if all you do is run down to the courthouse, while more elaborate elopements cost between $5,000 and $15,000 (https://www.brides.com/elopement-cost-5114438), most of which is used to pay for the photographer.

5.4 Pets: How Much They Cost and How to Save Money on Common Expenses

Setup Time	Maintenance Time	Function
N/A	N/A	Save Money

Pets bring joy, companionship, and . . . a whole bunch of unexpected expenses into our lives. From the obvious expenses, like food, grooming, and toys, to the not-so-obvious expenses, like figuring out an X-ray for my puppy who has a penchant for eating things he's not supposed to, costs go well over $500 (true story, not fun); getting a pet is a real financial responsibility.

Essential Terminology

Pet Insurance: Insurance coverage for your dog or cat designed to assist with the cost of veterinary care.

Ingredient List

Required:

- Initial savings to cover adoption fees and vet visits
- An emergency fund (see Section 1.3)
- Time to properly care for a pet

Optional:

- Budgeting tools
  - Download my free budgeting spreadsheet at nicktalksmoney .com/budget
  - See a list of my favorite budgeting apps at nicktalksmoney .com/budgetapps

Recipe

1. Understand the initial costs. Well before you plan to bring a pet into your home, start saving the money you'll need to cover adoption, toys, equipment, food, and vet bills.
   a. According to Petco, care for a puppy can cost between $900 and $2,500 in its first year (https://www.petco.com/content/ petco/PetcoStore/en_US/pet-services/resource-center/new-pet/puppy-cost-first-year.html), which doesn't include the breeder fee or cost of adoption.
   b. Also, according to Petco, the average kitten will drain your bank account between $1,331 and $3,334 in its first year (https://www.petco.com/content/petco/PetcoStore/en_US/ pet-services/resource-center/new-pet/budgeting-for-your-kittens-first-year.html), though this does include adoption/ breeder fees.
2. Build a robust emergency fund. In Section 1.3, we said an emergency fund should be equal to three to six months of your

necessary expenses. When you get a pet, this will also include their expenses, so a good rule of thumb is to bump up your emergency fund to six to nine months' worth of your current necessary expenses.

a. As I mentioned at the start of this section, my puppy had a few instances where he swallowed something he wasn't supposed to, so we had to take him to either the vet or ER to get X-rays done, and in one situation induce vomiting. Our pet insurance was of little help here (it only helps out above a certain dollar amount per visit, which just so happened to be about $100 more than the cost of an X-ray), so this led us to spend a cool $1,500 more than we were expecting during our puppy Bean's first year. If you don't have an emergency fund in place for these large, unexpected expenses, you may be forced to turn to a credit card for help, which is a slippery slope.

3. Based on your pet's breed and expected size, calculate your expected monthly food, treat, and toy expenditures, and factor those into your monthly budget. Large dogs, for example, will require more food and larger/sturdier toys (which are more expensive than smaller toys).

a. Dog food costs an average of $20 to $60 per month, though specialty diets can run more than $100 per month (https://www.portercountyanimalshelter.org/158/The-Costs-Of-Owning-A-Dog#:~:text=This%20typically%20costs%20some where%20from,%24100%20or%20more%20a%20month).

b. Cat food, on the other hand, only costs an average of $10 to $42 per month (https://www.hshv.org/cost-of-owning-a-cat/).

4. After you bring your new furry friend home, it's a good idea to immediately look into buying pet insurance for them. Bare minimum, this can financially protect you if your pet requires a multi-thousand-dollar procedure. In some cases, it can also help offset the costs of preventative care. Compare different pet insurance plans based on coverage options, deductibles (how much you have to pay out of pocket before the insurance company helps), and premiums (your monthly bill). It's like car

insurance: you hope you never have to use it, but if a situation arises where you need it, it can save you from *serious* financial strain.

    a. The average cost of pet insurance for dogs in 2023 is between $20 and $49 per month (https://www.valuepenguin.com/pet-insurance/average-cost-of-pet-insurance).

    b. The average cost of pet insurance for cats in 2023 is between $11 and $29 per month (https://www.valuepenguin.com/pet-insurance/average-cost-of-pet-insurance).

5. Don't always buy medication directly from your vet. Oftentimes, the same medication (or a generic version) can be found online for a fraction of the price. However, before you buy any medication online, clear it with your vet to ensure it's a safe option for your pet.

6. Try DIYing treats! Store-bought treats can be expensive and may contain a whole list of ingredients you can't even pronounce, so why not try to make a simple batch of treats yourself? As a personal finance book, this isn't the place to find recipe inspiration, but treats we like to make for my dog include frozen banana slices, baked sweet potato bites, pumpkin puree, and even just freezing peanut butter on a lick mat. Of course, before feeding anything to your pet, check to ensure it's safe for them to eat.

7. Above all else, ensure you enjoy your companionship with your pet!

Recap

1. Pets are an immense financial commitment: Ensure you have adequate savings for their first-year expenses (which will likely be the costliest year for them, outside of their later years) and a fully funded emergency fund.

2. Include your pet's estimated monthly expenses in your budget.

3. Look into pet insurance: It's a relatively cheap monthly payment that can protect you from being financially ruined if your pet requires an expensive procedure.

4. Consider opting for generic medication and making treats at home (both with your vet's approval, of course).

Chapter 6
College

6.1 How to Save Money on College While You're Still in High School

Setup Time	Maintenance Time	Function
4 Years	4 Years	Save Money

If you or your child is in high school, it's time to start thinking about college (if that's a path you/your child will take). The average cost of one academic year while attending an in-state public university in the USA is $26,027 in 2023, while the average cost of one academic year at a private university in the USA is $55,840 per year (https://educationdata.org/average-cost-of-college#:~:text=The%20average%20cost%20of%20attendance,or%20%24218%2C004%20over%204%20years). All-in, when considering student loan interest and the loss of income from not working full-time for four years, a bachelor's degree can ultimately cost over $500,000 (https://education data.org/average-cost-of-college#:~:text=The%20average%20cost%20of%20attendance,or%20%24218%2C004%20over%204%20years). Just as you might preemptively build your credit score to get a better deal on a house one day (see Section 3.4), you can preemptively take actions to save money on college tuition while you're still in high school.

Essential Terminology

Authorized User: An individual who is added to another person's credit card account. The authorized user will benefit from the primary cardholder's credit history and responsible credit usage (or they could suffer from poor credit usage, so be careful). Some cards have authorized user age limits (usually between 13 and 16 years old), while others don't.

Advanced Placement (AP) Classes: Classes taught in high schools that follow a curriculum established by the College Board. Upon completion of these classes, students must take a rigorous "AP Exam" on the topic covered in the class. If they score well on the exam, they could earn college credits that can let them skip introductory courses on the same topic in college, which saves you money on tuition. Note that each college/university has their own policies on AP credit acceptance, so it's important to understand the policies of the college you/your child is thinking of attending before enrolling for AP classes.

College in Schools (CIS): These are similar to AP classes, but instead of being taught a curriculum in a high school class that was approved by the College Board, high school students take actual college courses taught by approved high school instructors. Instead of needing to pass one ultimate AP exam after you complete the class, you simply need to achieve a grade above a certain threshold to acquire college credit. For example, I grew up in Minnesota, and my high school offered a CIS Calculus class based on the curriculum used at the University of Minnesota. I earned an A in the class, so I earned college credit and didn't need to take calculus when I enrolled at the University of Minnesota in the following year. Note that, just like AP classes, each higher education institution will have different rules on which CIS credits they'll accept, so it's wise to check on this before enrolling in a CIS class. Lucky for me, the CIS class I took was from the same institution I ended up attending, so there was no question it would be accepted.

Post-Secondary Enrollment Options (PSEO) (a.k.a. The Concurrent Enrollment Program, Dual Credit Program,

and many different names depending on the state): This is a step up from CIS classes, as this involves high school students directly taking classes at local colleges or universities alongside full-time college students. High school students participating in PSEO earn both high school and college credit (at zero cost to them), reducing the time (and, in turn, money) it takes to earn a college degree. For example, my younger brother was a full-time PSEO student during his senior year of high school, so he was able to jump right into 2nd-year classes during his freshman year of college. This allowed him to graduate college a full year early, saving more than $20,000 that fourth year of college would've cost him. As with every other program on this list, every college or university has different rules regarding what they'll accept for transfer credits, so it's important to check this out ahead of time.

Ingredient List

Required:

- A child willing to push themselves academically
- A high school that offers AP, CIS, or PSEO programs

Optional:

- A parent/guardian with an excellent credit score

Recipe

Note: To avoid constantly switching perspectives, the recipe is written as if speaking to a high school student, not their parent/guardian.

1. Start building your credit score. If you have a parent, guardian, or even close relative who has an excellent credit score, ask if you can be added as an "authorized user" on their credit card. This will build your credit history, and on-time payments made by the account owner will also positively impact your credit score. Building a good credit score this early is important because it can

help you get the lowest interest rates on student loans, meaning it could potentially save you a lot of money.

    a. However, beware that poor credit habits (like missing payments) by the account owner can also hurt the authorized user's credit score. If you have to choose between not building your credit score or being added as an authorized user on someone's account with poor credit management, I'd choose not to build your credit score.

2. Take academics seriously. In order to qualify for the programs we listed under essential terminology (we'll cover them in a minute), you typically need to meet certain GPA criteria. Don't let a D– you got in the music class freshman year because you were goofing around be the reason you can't enroll in an AP class (and potentially save thousands of dollars on college tuition).

3. Enroll in AP classes. Assuming your high school offers them, these are typically the first type of college credit–earning classes you're allowed to enroll in, with many being made available to high school sophomores. It's important to stay engaged and take effective notes throughout the whole school year, because whether or not you earn college credit for the class comes down to its AP exam at the end of the year.

4. If you demonstrate success with these AP classes, along with your standard high school classes, you may become eligible to enroll in CIS classes. As mentioned in their description, the coursework for these classes may be a bit more rigorous than AP classes (because it's an actual college curriculum), but as long as you earn a certain grade in the class, you earn college credit. You don't need to stress about an all-or-nothing final exam (though a final exam will likely still carry significant weight on your grade). CIS classes allow high school juniors and seniors to earn college credit while still going through the typical high school "experience," since all these classes are taught at your high school, by high school teachers, and all your classmates will be fellow students at your high school.

5. If you want to maximize your college credit earning, explore your school's PSEO offerings (note that the names of these programs vary widely by state, but many states offer something similar).

This allows high school students to become either part-time or full-time students of a local higher education institution, at zero cost to them. This means, if you are a full-time PSEO student for your junior and senior years of high school, you could potentially graduate college two years early, which means you'd save two years of college costs. However, this could obviously impact your high school experience, as you'd be physically taking classes at a college instead of at your high school. This will limit your interactions with your high school friends and, depending on the timing of your classes, could hinder your ability to participate in school sports.

   a. If this is something you're interested in pursuing, you need to get in touch with your high school's guidance counselor. Note that a PSEO program may have GPA requirements, or require that you obtain a minimum score on a standardized test.

Recap

1. If you have a parent, guardian, or relative with an excellent credit score, ask to be added as an authorized user on their credit card. This can build your credit score, which can reduce the cost of student loans.
2. Try hard in school, and take AP, CIS, and PSEO classes, if available.

6.2   How to Apply for Grants

Setup Time	Maintenance Time	Function
5–20 Hours	N/A	Save Money

Newsflash: college is *expensive*. The average cost of one academic year while attending an in-state public university in the USA is $26,027 in 2023, while the average cost of one academic year at a private university in the USA is $55,840 per year (https://education data.org/average-cost-of-college#:~:text=The%20average%20 cost%20of%20attendance,or%20%24218%2C004%20over%204% 20years). Section 6.1 shows you how to save money on tuition by earning college credits in high school, but this recipe will show you how to apply for a form of financial assistance called "grants."

Essential Terminology

College Grants: Money given to students to support their educational expenses. Grants can be offered by federal and state governments, as well as private sources. They're awarded based on a number of criteria specific to each grant, but common criteria include academic merit and financial need. Grants are usually "free" to the recipient: You aren't charged interest on them and don't need to pay them back. However, in some circumstances, a grant may come with certain criteria that must be met, otherwise it must be repaid like a student loan.

FAFSA: The Free Application for Federal Student Aid (FAFSA) is something that nearly every college student needs to complete annually because it's what qualifies them for federal student aid. This includes federal student loans, work study programs, and—you guessed it—federal grants.

Ingredient List

Required:

- Computer or smartphone
- Financial information for the student and family (tax returns, pay stubs)
- Social Security number or ITIN (student and family)

Recipe

Note: To avoid constantly switching perspectives, the recipe is written as if speaking to a high school student, not their parent/guardian.

1. **Complete the FAFSA:** It's available starting October 1st of the year before you plan to attend college (and you complete it every year around this time as long as you plan to attend college the following year). Even though the FAFSA deadline isn't until the following June 30th, completing it as early as possible gives you the best chance to secure grants because many financial aid programs are distributed on a first come, first served basis (https://studentaid.gov/articles/10-fafsa-mistakes-to-avoid/).

2. Search and apply for grants using:
   a. www.careeronestop.org (Navigate to "toolkit," then click "scholarship finder." You can sort by "grant" under "Award Type" to only see grants.)
   b. bigfuture.collegeboard.org/ (Navigate to "Pay for College," then select "Scholarship Search." You can search for both scholarships and grants with this tool.)

3. Search around for harder-to-find grants offered by your high school, organizations in your community, or even by your parents' workplaces. The harder a grant is to find, the less competition you'll have for it.

4. Before applying for grants, prepare all the standard information you'll need to submit along with them. This could include high school/college transcripts, recommendation letters, personal statements, and proof of eligibility (for grants targeting certain demographics or fields of study).

5. Apply, apply, apply. It may feel tedious writing dozens of application essays, but you have to think about what your hourly rate is for this work. If you spend 100 hours applying for grants, and are "only" approved for one totaling $10,000, that's an average rate of $100/hour. How fast would you jump at a job that's offering you $100/hour?

6. Pay attention to application deadlines, and, if you haven't heard anything from an organization after a couple of weeks, follow up with them (via email if you submitted your application electronically, or via physical mail if you mailed in your application). Restate your interest in the grant, and kindly ask when they believe they'll have an update by. This bonus step of

taking initiative will put you at the top of their minds and may be the extra little bit of motivation that's needed to award you the grant.

7. When approved for grants, carefully review their offers for:
   a. Award amount
   b. Duration (is it $5,000 over one year or over four years?)
   c. Renewal requirements
   d. Additional obligations or restrictions (like GPA requirements)
8. Accept all the grants you feel comfortable with and attend college knowing that you saved yourself a ton of money!
   a. Note: You can, and should, continue to apply for grants throughout your time at college. Again, it's hard to find a job with as good of an hourly rate as applying for grants.

Recap

1. Complete the FAFSA on October 1st of the year before your first (or next) year of college starts. This will be used to see if you qualify for federal and institution-specific (from your college) grants.
2. Search and apply for as many additional grant opportunities as possible using www.careeronestop.org and bigfuture.college board.org/.
3. Follow-up on your grant applications.
4. Understand and approve your grant offers.

6.3   How to Apply for Scholarships

Setup Time	Maintenance Time	Function
5–20 Hours	N/A	Save Money

Scholarships, along with grants (Section 6.2), are among the most well-known forms of college financial aid. While scholarships and grants share some similarities, they also have their fair share of differences. However, both can be key pieces of your college payment plan, assuming you'd rather not pay the entire $26,027, which is the average cost of one academic year while attending an in-state public university in the USA in 2023, out of pocket (https:// educationdata.org/average-cost-of-college#:~:text=The%20average %20cost%20of%20attendance,or%20%24218%2C004%20over% 204%20years).

Essential Terminology

Scholarships: Financial awards given to students to help (or fully) cover education expenses. Scholarships can be awarded by colleges, foundations, organizations, and even philanthropic individuals. Eligibility ranges greatly depend on the criteria of each scholarship, but common categories include academic merit, athletics, community involvement, financial need, or specific talents (such as music).

Ingredient List

Required:

- Computer or smartphone
- Transcripts and letters of recommendation (often, but not always, required)

Recipe

Note: To avoid constantly switching perspectives, the recipe is written as if speaking to a high school student, not their parent/guardian.

1. Start your scholarship search earlier than you think you need to. Many scholarships have deadlines months in advance of a school year starting, which you don't want to miss out on due to procrastination.
2. Search and apply for scholarships using websites like:
   a. www.careeronestop.org (Navigate to "toolkit," then click "scholarship finder." You can sort by "scholarship" under "Award Type" to only see scholarships.)

b. bigfuture.collegeboard.org/ (Navigate to "Pay for College," then select "Scholarship Search." You can search for both scholarships and grants with this tool.)

3. Search around for harder-to-find scholarships offered by organizations in your community, your workplace, or even by your parents' workplaces. The harder a scholarship is to find, the less competition you'll have for it.

4. Before applying for scholarships, prepare all the standard information you'll need to submit along with them. This could include high school/college transcripts, recommendation letters, and personal statements.

5. Apply, apply, apply. It may feel tedious writing dozens of application essays, but you have to think about what your hourly rate is for this work: If you spend 100 hours applying for scholarships, and are "only approved for one totaling $10,000, that's an average rate of $100/hour. How fast would you jump at a job that's offering you $100/hour?

6. Pay attention to application deadlines, and, if you haven't heard anything from an organization after a couple weeks, follow up with them (via email if you submitted your application electronically, via physical mail if you mailed in your application). Restate your interest in the scholarship, and kindly ask when they believe they'll have an update by. This bonus step of taking initiative will put you at the top of their minds, and may be the extra little bit of motivation that's needed to award you the scholarship.

7. When approved for scholarships, carefully review their offers for:
   a. Award amount
   b. Duration (is it $5,000 over one year or over four years?)
   c. Renewal requirements (such as maintaining a certain GPA)
   d. Additional obligations or restrictions

8. Accept all the scholarships you feel comfortable with and attend college knowing that you saved yourself a ton of money!
   a. Note: You can, and should, continue to apply for scholarships throughout your time at college. Again, it's hard to find a job with as good of an hourly rate as applying for scholarships.

Recap

1. Search and apply for as many scholarship opportunities as possible using www.careeronestop.org and bigfuture.collegeboard.org/.
2. Follow up on your scholarship applications.
3. Understand and approve your scholarship offers.

6.4 How to Make College a Good Investment

Setup Time	Maintenance Time	Function
4 Years	4 Years	Make Money

The prospect of spending four years of your life and more than $100,000 to attend college can make you question whether college is even worth it. Well, on average, it is: The average college graduate makes $1.2 million more than the average high school–only graduate over their lifetimes (https://www.aplu.org/our-work/4-policy-and-advocacy/publicuvalues/employment-earnings/#:~:text=College%20graduates%20are%20half%20as,million%20more%20over%20their%20lifetime.), and the median salary for college graduates aged 22–27 was $22,000 per year higher than high school–only graduates in the same age range in 2021 (https://www.aplu.org/our-work/4-policy-and-advocacy/publicuvalues/employment-earnings/#:~:text=The%20earnings%20gap%20between%20college,earnings%20are%20%2430%2C000%20a%20year). However, this doesn't mean that college is a good investment for *everyone*: We've all heard the horror stories of college graduates who racked up a mountain of student loan debt only to enter the real world unable to find a job in their field. College is an investment. This recipe will teach you how to make it a profitable one.

Essential Terminology

Scholarships: Financial awards given to students to help (or fully) cover education expenses. Scholarships can be awarded by colleges, foundations, organizations, and even philanthropic individuals. Eligibility ranges greatly depend on the criteria of each scholarship, but common categories include academic merit, athletics, community involvement, financial need, or specific talents (such as music).

College Grants: Money given to students to support their educational expenses. Grants can be offered by federal and state governments, as well as private sources. They're awarded based on a number of criteria specific to each grant, but common criteria include academic merit and financial need. Grants are usually "free" to the recipient: You aren't charged interest on them and don't need to pay them back. However, in some circumstances, a grant may come with certain criteria that must be met, otherwise it must be repaid like a student loan.

Major: Your primary field of study in college. Think Finance, English, Electrical Engineering, etc.

Internship: Essentially a "trial run" with a company. They come in both paid and unpaid forms and allow you to experience what working at a certain company in your desired area of study is like. They're typically for a set amount of time, with summer being the most popular since students don't have classes. This is a great way to earn a full-time offer from a company that you want to start a career with, and it's also a great way to see if a company, or even the entire field you're pursuing, is the right fit for you.

Networking: Building relationships that may eventually have a positive impact on your career.

Ingredient List

Required:

- A commitment to making college a good investment

Recipe

1. Choose the right college or university for you. Because private universities cost almost $30,000 more than public universities

per year, on average (https://educationdata.org/average-cost-of-college#:~:text=The%20average%20cost%20of%20attendance, or%20%24218%2C004%20over%204%20years.), it often doesn't make financial sense to attend them unless you receive a significant amount in scholarships/grants (ensure they aren't just frontloaded in the first year or two to make tuition look more affordable right away) or it's an extremely prestigious institution, like an Ivy League member, that would grant you access to career opportunities you simply wouldn't get as a student at a public university.

   a. Also realize that it's not just a battle between public and private universities: You could also choose to go to a community college or trade school. Community college tuition can be as little as $3,500 per year (https://www.nshss.org/blog/community-college-vs-university-pros-and-cons-of-cost-class-size-and-student-experience/), and many public universities accept credits from local community colleges. A popular cost-saving method is to attend community college long enough to complete your general classes (one to two years), then transfer to a public university to complete your major coursework (and gain the ability to tell future employers that you graduated from "The university of ___" instead of a community college). However, this method will definitely provide you with less of "the college experience" and hinder your networking ability since core college friend groups are often formed during freshman year.

2. Maximize scholarships and grants, they're literally free money. The lower the college costs for you, the easier it'll be to make it a good investment. See Sections 6.2 and 6.3 for more information on how to find and apply for them.

3. Choose a major that intersects with your interests and market demand. For example, someone who likes writing may want to major in marketing over a broader subject like English, because there are many more job prospects for marketing majors. If you want to further study a field that has little market demand, like theater or history, make that a minor, or even a double major with

a more practical major. In general, majors in the STEM (science, technology, engineering, mathematics) fields, finance, computer science, and healthcare tend to have the highest earning potential.

4. Make as many friends as possible in your area of study. This may be the only time in your life that you're surrounded by hundreds, if not thousands, of people trying to pursue a career similar to yours. Take advantage of this opportunity; you never know when a connection will help you further your career, or when you'll get the opportunity to help one of your connections further their career. Networking can be made easier by joining major-specific groups, clubs, intramural sports, and even fraternities and sororities.

   a. Don't limit your networking to only fellow students: get to know your professors and the company representatives who show up to on-campus career fairs. Your professors are likely very well connected, and, obviously, company representatives can help you land a job at their company.

5. Speaking of landing a job, try to get an internship related to your field of study every summer between school years. This will (probably) make you good money while exploring whether the company, or the field in general, is the right fit for you. Even if you don't land, or want, a full-time job with the company you interned for, it's a valuable experience you can throw on your resume that will put you leaps and bounds ahead of someone else whose only work experience is at the campus coffee shop when applying for jobs or future internships.

   a. Much like student aid, you should start applying for these well ahead of time. When I was in school, most internships sought by business school students interviewed and accepted interns the fall before their summer internship was set to start.

Recap

1. Apply for as many scholarships and grants as possible. The less college costs, the easier it'll be to make it a good investment.
2. Make a very conscious decision about whether you'll attend a public university, private university, community college, or trade school. Understand all the costs and benefits associated with each.

3. Choose a major that intersects with your interests and market demand. If you want to study something that doesn't have great job prospects, make it your minor.
4. Network your tail off with fellow students, professors, and company representatives at on-campus job fairs.
5. Make it a point to land internships relevant to your major every summer between school years.

6.5 How to Use a 529 Plan to Save for Your Kid's College

Setup Time	Maintenance Time	Function
30–45 Minutes	10 Minutes per Month	Save/Make Money

If you're a parent (or plan to be one day) who wants to help their kids pay for college, it's hard to find a better place to save up college funds than a 529 plan. This recipe will teach you what a 529 plan is, and walk you through how to set up and properly utilize one.

Essential Terminology

529 Plan: A tax-advantaged investing account that helps families save for education expenses. The tax advantages offered by 529 plans are similar to those offered by Roth IRAs (Section 2.2): You don't receive a federal tax deduction for funds contributed in the current year (though some states offer state tax deductions), but the funds inside of your 529 plan account grow tax free, and they can be withdrawn tax free to pay for "qualified education expenses."

Qualified Education Expenses: Expenses that can be paid for with tax-free distributions from a 529 plan, as long as the student is enrolled on at least a half-time basis. Examples include: tuition, school fees, books, supplies, required equipment, and room and board (within reason).

Ingredient List

Required:

- Computer or smartphone
- A child that may want to attend college someday
- Social Security number or ITIN for both you and your child

Recipe

1. Research 529 plans. The interesting thing about 529 plans is that most states offer their own, but you don't need to enroll in your home state's 529 plan. However, many states offer residents a state tax deduction on contributions made into their home state's 529 plan, so it may be worth it to stick with your home state as your 529 plan provider. Your child's potential school choices will not be impacted by which state you choose to open their 529 plan in.
   a. Ensure you open a "529 Education Savings Plan," not a "529 Prepaid Tuition Plan." The prepaid tuition plan lets you buy tuition credits at today's prices for an in-state, public college. Assuming you want to give your child a choice on where they attend college, it's best to move forward with an education savings plan.
2. Compare the 529s you find based on criteria like:
   a. Investment choices
   b. Fees
   c. Performance history
   d. User interface
   e. Available features
   f. Tax savings (if offered by your home state)
3. Once a 529 plan provider is chosen, navigate to their website and submit an account application. You'll need to provide personal information for both you and your child.
4. Make a contribution plan. As a rule of thumb, the earlier in your child's life that you start contributing to their 529 plan the lower your monthly contribution needs to be. Estimate the cost of

college for your child, then use a compound interest calculator (a web search of that term will give you plenty to choose from) to determine how much money you need to contribute to fully pay for their college. Or, maybe you only want to pay for part of their college, and you base your contributions around that.

   a. What happens if your child decides not to attend college, or they have leftover money in their 529 plan after they're done with college? You have two options: 1) you could transfer that money to another beneficiary's 529 plan (like another one of your children or a niece/nephew), or 2) starting in 2024, up to $35,000 from a 529 plan that has been open for at least fifteen years can be rolled into a Roth IRA tax and penalty free.

5. Decide what to invest in. The most common investment choice inside of 529 plans is an age-based target date fund: This means that, when the child is younger, a greater percentage of the investment portfolio is allocated toward higher-risk assets like index funds and stocks (which have a high potential for growth), but as the child gets closer to college age, the fund will shift to a more conservative investing philosophy, opting to invest in more stable assets like bonds (much less upside, but also much less downside). Picking a target date fund means you can essentially set it and forget it: Outside of an annual review to make sure everything is running smoothly, you won't need to actively manage the 529 plan.

   a. See Section 2.5 for a longer explanation on index funds and bonds.

6. As the years pass by, monitor the 529 plan balance to ensure you aren't overfunding it. However, if you have multiple children, you don't need to worry as much about overfunding, because, as we mentioned in Step 4, excess funds can simply be passed down to the next child.

7. When your child reaches college age, funds from the 529 plan can be withdrawn tax free to pay for qualified education expenses.

8. As mentioned in Step 4, once your child has completed their education (including undergraduate and graduate school, if they

choose to continue their education), you have two choices for what to do with the leftover balance: 1) you could transfer that money to another beneficiary's 529 plan (like another one of your children or a niece/nephew), or 2) starting in 2024, up to $35,000 from a 529 plan that has been open for at least fifteen years can be rolled into a Roth IRA tax and penalty free.

Recap

1. Choose a 529 plan provider based on potential tax deductions, investment choices, fees, and user experience.
2. Set a contribution goal, and start automatic monthly contributions to reach it.
3. Decide how this money is invested; age-based target date funds are the most popular investment choice for 529 plans.
4. When your child reaches college age, funds from the 529 plan can be withdrawn tax free to pay for qualified education expenses.
5. If there are any funds left over in the 529 plan after your child has finished their higher education, either 1) transfer that money to another beneficiary's 529 plan (like another one of your children or a niece/nephew), or 2) starting in 2024, up to $35,000 from a 529 plan that has been open for at least fifteen years can be rolled into a Roth IRA tax and penalty free.

6.6   How to Pay Off Your Student Loans

Setup Time	Maintenance Time	Function
30–45 Minutes	10 Minutes per Month	Debt Payoff

So you went to college but weren't lucky enough to have parents who paid for everything with a 529 plan (see Section 6.5), so you graduated with around the national average of $33,500 in student

loans (https://educationdata.org/average-student-loan-debt#:~:
text=University%20graduates%20owe%20an%20average,
For%2Dprofit%20students%20borrow%20%2449%2C700). What's the
best way to pay them off? That entirely depends on your situation,
but we'll cover the three most common repayment methods for federal student loans in this recipe.

*Note: If you have significantly more debt than the $33.5k average,
especially if a portion of it is private student loans, you may want to
pursue the more aggressive debt payoff methods described in Chapter 4.*

Essential Terminology

Repayment Plan: This determines how much your monthly loan
payments are and how long you'll make them. The three most
common types of repayment plans for federal student loans are:
standard, income-driven, and extended.

Standard Repayment Plan: You make a fixed monthly payment
over ten years, after which your debt will be fully paid off. As its
name suggests, this is the default repayment option for federal student loans.

Income-Driven Repayment (IDR) Plans: IDRs adjust your
monthly payments based on your income and family size, which
should make your loan payments more manageable than they
would be under a standard repayment plan.

Extended Repayment Plan: As the name suggests, extended
repayment plans can extend the repayment term well beyond the
standard 10-year period. On higher loan balances, you could stretch
your payments out over a period of up to twenty-five years. While
this will lower your monthly payments, extending your payment
time horizon will lead to you paying more interest over the life of
your loans.

Grace Period: The period of time after you graduate, leave school,
or drop below half-time enrollment when you are not required to
make loan payments. The exact timing depends on your loan and
lender, but it's typically around six months.

Ingredient List

Required:

- Loan account information

Optional:

- Budgeting tools
  - Download my free budgeting spreadsheet at nicktalksmoney
    .com/budget
  - See a list of my favorite budgeting apps at nicktalksmoney
    .com/budgetapps
- More aggressive debt payoff methods (see Chapter 4)

Recipe

1. Research and choose a repayment plan. After you graduate college, leave school, or drop below half-time enrollment, you usually have around a six-month grace period before you're required to make student loan payments. During this time, it's important to log in to your student loan servicer (their name will be on your student loan statements; common federal loan servicers include Nelnet, MOHELA, and Navient) and choose a repayment plan. The three most common repayment plans are:
   a. **Standard Repayment Plan**: You'll make fixed monthly payments for ten years, after which your loans will be paid off.
   b. **Income-Driven Repayment Plan**: Your monthly payments are adjusted based on your income and family size.
   c. **Extended Repayment Plan**: Depending on your loan amount, payments could be stretched out as long as 25 years. This plan will come with the lowest monthly payments, but will also lead you to pay the most interest.
2. Decide whether to make additional payments toward your student loans. If you chose the standard repayment plan, you may have additional money you can put toward paying off your loans early every month. Whether this makes sense for you depends

on two factors: 1) the interest rates of your loans and 2) your risk tolerance. If your loans have relatively low interest rates (a benchmark I use is under 6%), over a long enough period of time, you may reasonably expect to earn more than 6% by investing that extra money in the stock market (which has had an average annual return of over 11% since 1950 [https://www.officialdata.org/us/stocks/s-p-500/1950?amount=100&end Year=2023]), so opportunity cost dictates that you should invest your extra money instead of using it to pay off your loans early. However, the stock market is wildly unpredictable in the short-term, and you may feel immense peace of mind by paying off your loans early, so this is a deeply personal decision.

3. When your repayment plan begins, ensure you turn on autopay so you never accidentally miss a payment.
4. Establish an emergency fund (Section 1.3) to further ensure you never miss a loan payment.
5. If your loan situation feels insurmountable, especially if you have private student loans, consider the more aggressive debt repayment tactics discussed in Chapter 4.

Recap

1. After you graduate college, choose one of the three main repayment plans for your student loans.
2. Based on your loans' interest rates and your own personal risk tolerance, decide whether to invest any extra cash flow or use it to pay off your loans early.
3. Activate autopay and establish an emergency fund (Section 1.3) to ensure you never miss a loan payment.
4. If your loan situation feels insurmountable, especially if you have private student loans, consider the more aggressive debt repayment tactics discussed in Chapter 4.

Chapter 7
Housing

7.1 Is It Better for You to Rent or Buy a House?

Setup Time	Maintenance Time	Function
30 Minutes	N/A, Unless You Work with a Real Estate Agent/Mortgage Broker	Lifestyle

> You really need to stop throwing away money on rent.
> —*your parents, who paid $5.82 for their 4-bedroom*
> *home back when they were your age*

The decision between buying and renting a place to live is, undoubtedly, one of the largest financial decisions you'll make in your entire life. This recipe will guide you through the pros and cons of each option to ensure you don't make a rash decision to buy, just because that's the conventionally "smart" thing to do, and end up house poor.

Essential Terminology

House Poor: When a homebuyer, intentionally or unintentionally, buys a house that is too expensive to comfortably fit in their budget. Individuals that are house poor spend a significant portion of their income on mortgage payments, property taxes, insurance, and maintenance costs, which leads them to struggle with meeting other financial wants and needs.

Down Payment: The initial cash lump sum you need to pay when buying a house. "Standard" down payments equal 20% of a home's purchase price, though first-time homebuyers can put as little as 3.5% down if they qualify for an FHA loan.

Mortgage: A loan to buy a house; the house itself serves as collateral for the loan. This means, if you fail to make your loan payments, the bank that issued your mortgage could potentially take ownership of your home.

Ingredient List

Required:

- A clear view of your long-term goals
- Market research

Optional:

- Real estate agent
- Mortgage pre-approval
- Buying vs renting calculator (a web search will yield plenty of great results)

Recipe

1. Intentionally think about where and how you see yourself living in the near future. If you're unsure of where you want to live, buying doesn't make sense because of the massive amount of transaction fees and effort it takes to buy and sell a home. Also, when you buy a home, you're responsible for fixing everything that goes wrong with the home. If you rent, the most you have to worry about is keeping your place tidy, and even that is technically optional.
2. Analyze the financial aspect, and make sure it's more than comparing your potential mortgage to your current rent payments.

When you buy a home, your mortgage is the *minimum* you'll spend each month (along with maintenance, home improvements, insurance, utilities, and taxes), while your rent is the *maximum* you'll spend each month. Not only that, but you have to take into account the opportunity cost of paying a down payment vs investing that money instead. There are plenty of rent vs buy payment calculators on the internet you can play around with. Realize that buying more house than you can afford has a real chance at making you house poor.

3. Analyze the lifestyle factors. Most of my fellow financial planners tend to agree that buying a personal residence isn't necessarily a wise financial decision: You'd typically see better returns by renting and investing your excess money into the stock market. However, a multitude of lifestyle factors, such as securing a place in a good school system, the ability to customize your living space, and being able to put down real roots in a community can all be great reasons to opt for buying a house.

4. If you're on the fence, contact a mortgage broker to get pre-approved for a loan. This will show you what your expected mortgage payments would be if you bought a home. To take it one step further, you could even work with a real estate agent to see what sort of homes are available, and get a glimpse at the current market dynamics (whether it's favorable to buyers or sellers). Mortgage brokers and real estate agents only get paid if you end up buying a house with them, so this process will be completely free otherwise.

Recap

1. Have a clear vision of the lifestyle you want to live for the next five to ten years.
2. Determine whether you can even afford to buy in current market conditions.
3. If you're on the fence, work with a mortgage broker and real estate agent to get a clear look at how much a home will cost you and what options are available.

7.2   How to Tell If Rent/Your Mortgage Payment Is Too Expensive for Your Income Level

Setup Time	Maintenance Time	Function
30 Minutes	N/A	Manage Money

"A household's single largest expense is housing" (https://nhc.org/wp-content/uploads/2017/03/p2p-2015-sup.pdf), so it's important not to overextend yourself and become house poor. This recipe will help you determine how much of your budget you can reasonably spend on housing.

Essential Terminology

House Poor: When a homebuyer, intentionally or unintentionally, buys a house that is too expensive to comfortably fit in their budget. Individuals that are house poor spend a significant portion of their income on mortgage payments, property taxes, insurance, and maintenance costs, which leads them to struggle with meeting other financial wants and needs.

Ingredient List

Required:

- Knowledge of your monthly income
- Knowledge of current, and/or potential future, housing costs

Optional:

- Budgeting Tools
  - Download my free budgeting spreadsheet at nicktalksmoney.com/budget

- See a list of my favorite budgeting apps at nicktalksmoney .com/budgetapps

Recipe

1. Calculate your total take-home income during an average month. This can include earnings from a job, side hustle, and investments. Ensure this number is listed after taxes. If you are living with somebody else, like a spouse or roommate, add their income here too.
   a. Using one of the listed budgeting tools will help you calculate this number.
2. Multiply this take-home income number by 30%—this is the rent/mortgage amount that financial planners would recommend you don't exceed.
3. Compare this number with your current rent/mortgage: If your housing expenses are above this number, you may want to think about finding a less costly living situation to create more room in your budget. Alternatively, you could also increase your income to raise your affordability threshold. If your housing costs are below 30% of your take-home income, congratulations! You're living below your means.
4. However, before you take any drastic action, plug your maximum housing cost into your total budget: Depending on how your other income is used, maybe you can spend a little bit more than 30% on housing, or vice versa if your budget is already pretty tight.

Recap

1. Multiply your monthly take-home income by 30% to find your maximum monthly housing budget.
2. See if this number makes sense based on your overall budget.
3. Make changes to your housing situation, if needed.

7.3   How to Buy Your First House

Setup Time	Maintenance Time	Function
3–5 Hours	Many Hours per Month Until You Close on a House	Home Buying

So, you've decided to buy your first house. The only problem? You've been taught *nothing* about the home buying process, so you have no idea where to start. This recipe will walk you through the steps required to become a homeowner.

Essential Terminology

Down Payment: The initial cash lump sum you need to pay when buying a house. "Standard" down payments equal 20% of a home's purchase price, though first-time homebuyers can put as little as 3.5% down if they qualify for an FHA loan.

Mortgage: A loan to buy a house; the house itself serves as collateral for the loan. This means, if you fail to make your loan payments, the bank that issued your mortgage could potentially take ownership of your home.

Closing Costs: Fees and expenses that must be paid to the different parties in a real estate transaction when buying a home. Closing costs can include lender fees, appraisal costs, title insurance, and real estate agent fees.

Pre-approval: The process of being approved for a mortgage before you've found a house to buy. Your lender will evaluate your financial situation and approve you for a loan up to a certain amount. Getting pre-approved gives you a clear picture of what price range of homes you should consider and strengthens your position as a serious buyer.

Ingredient List

Required:

- A solid financial foundation
- Cash savings for a down payment and closing costs
- A mortgage lender
- A real estate agent

  Optional

- A high-yield savings account (HYSA) to hold your down payment and closing cost funds
  - See a list of my favorite HYSAs at nicktalksmoney.com/HYSA

Recipe

1. Before you even think about buying a home, ensure you've built a stable financial foundation for yourself. This means you:
   a. Have a steady stream of income
   b. Have a fully funded emergency fund (see Section 1.3)
   c. Don't have any high-interest debt (see Chapter 4)
   d. Have a good credit score (see Section 3.4)
   e. Have plenty of breathing room in your budget (see Section 1.4)
2. Save for a down payment and closing costs. A "normal" down payment is 20% of a home's purchase price, so the down payment on a $500,000 home would be $100,000. However, first-time homebuyers may qualify for down payments as low as 3.5% (or 0% if you're a veteran): Talk to your mortgage lender about specifics. Just keep in mind that the higher your down payment is, the lower your monthly mortgage payment will be. An additional 2% to 5% of the home's purchase price should also be budgeted for closing costs.
   a. You'll be saving up a significant amount of cash here; make sure it earns interest for you in the meantime by keeping it in something like a high-yield savings account (see Section 1.2).

3. Get pre-approved for a mortgage. Reach out to several different mortgage lenders in your area and request pre-approval for a mortgage. Having a multitude of options will often lead to receiving more favorable interest rates on your loan (many offer price-matching if you find a loan with a lower interest rate). At this step, you can also discuss your different loan and down payment options with your lender. Getting pre-approved doesn't cost you anything: The mortgage lender only gets paid if you buy a home with their loan.

4. Interview a handful of real estate agents that specialize in the area where you want to buy a home. Personal referrals are the best way to find good agents, but your lenders will almost certainly be able to provide you with contact info for their favorite agents otherwise. I highly recommend using a real estate agent, especially when buying your first home. They have intimate knowledge of the market, know the ins and outs of negotiating, and may even have access to off-market deals. Like mortgage lenders, they don't get paid unless you buy a home through them.

5. Your real estate agent will then take you through the process of touring potential properties.

6. When you find properties that you like, your agent will help you write an offer on them. This doesn't automatically mean that you'll get the house, as there are likely other prospective buyers, and, even if there aren't, the seller will probably try to get you to raise your purchase price regardless through negotiations. However, this is where a good real estate agent will shine: They'll handle the bulk of the negotiations with the seller, and may even earn some concessions (a.k.a. a discount) for things like repairs.

7. After your offer is accepted, you'll enter the "due diligence" phase. This is a period when you are allowed to conduct inspections on the property and, if you don't like what you see, you can typically back out for little-to-no cost.

8. If the inspections come back clean, you'll finalize financing with your lender and close the deal. This is when closing costs (typically 2% to 5% of the home price) are due, so don't get caught off guard by them.

Recap

1. Build a strong financial foundation before even thinking about buying a house.
2. Save up enough money for a down payment and closing costs inside of an HYSA.
3. Get pre-approved for a mortgage with a lender and interview real estate agents.
4. Tour and submit offers on properties with the real estate agent you chose.
5. Negotiate and close on deals with the help of your real estate agent.

7.4 How to Decide Between a 15-Year vs 30-Year Mortgage

Setup Time	Maintenance Time	Function
30 Minutes	N/A	Home Buying

As you learned if you read Section 7.3, you'll need to get a mortgage if you plan on buying a house (unless you happen to have enough cash lying around to buy it outright). One of the biggest decisions you need to make when choosing a mortgage, along with the size of the down payment, is the length of the mortgage. The two most common options are 15 and 30 years; this recipe will walk you through the pros and cons of each.

Essential Terminology

Mortgage: A loan to buy a house; the house itself serves as collateral for the loan. This means, if you fail to make your loan payments, the bank that issued your mortgage could potentially take ownership of your home.

Mortgage Term: The duration of your mortgage. The most common terms are 15 and 30 years, though other options may be available.

Interest Rate: How much the lender charges you for borrowing funds. The higher your interest rate, the higher your monthly payment will be.

Down Payment: The initial cash lump sum you need to pay when buying a house. "Standard" down payments equal 20% of a home's purchase price, though first-time homebuyers can put as little as 3.5% down if they qualify for an FHA loan.

Ingredient List

Required:

- A mortgage lender
- Knowledge of your personal finances
- Mortgage calculators (a web search will provide plenty of useful results)

Recipe

1. Intimately understand your current financial situation and what the maximum amount you can spend on housing expenses each month would be.
2. Get pre-approved by multiple different lenders; this will let you find a lender offering the lowest interest rates.
3. Ask your lender to run projections for the monthly cost of both a 15- and 30-year mortgage at your expected home purchase price and down payment.
4. Evaluate your options. A 15-year mortgage will come with higher monthly payments, but you'll pay off your home 15 years earlier, which will save you a significant amount of interest. A 30-year mortgage will have lower monthly payments, which will give you more flexibility in your budget, but your payments will continue over a much longer time horizon, and you'll pay significantly more interest than a 15-year mortgage.
   a. It's important to factor in opportunity cost here as well: The lower payments of a 30-year mortgage will allow you to invest more money into the stock market in the meantime, which diversifies your assets. A 15-year mortgage may not

leave you with enough breathing room to invest, so your
entire net worth could be tied up in your house.

5. If you're still on the fence, run different saving/investing scenarios for each mortgage on one of the dozens of calculators you can find online for this very topic; just search "15- vs 30-year mortgage calculator," and also include a "compound interest calculator" to see how much your extra invested funds could grow.

Recap

1. Have an intimate knowledge of your budget and how much can be allocated toward monthly housing expenses.
2. Shop around for mortgages with multiple lenders to find the lowest interest rates.
3. Ask your lender to run projections for the monthly cost of both a 15- and 30-year mortgage at your expected home purchase price and down payment.
4. Evaluate your options, including the assumption that you could potentially invest your excess money if it's not all being put toward a mortgage payment.

7.5 How to Reduce Your Living Expenses by House Hacking

Setup Time	Maintenance Time	Function
Greatly Varies	Varies Depending on Your Tenants	Save and Make Money

If you followed the recipe to buy a home outlined in Section 7.3, but realized that buying a home may seem to be a bit out of your budget right now, you may want to consider house hacking. House hacking allows you to significantly reduce your living expenses, or even potentially generate income from a property that you own and are living in. This recipe will walk you through the process of house hacking.

Essential Terminology

House Hacking: Living in one part of a property, while generating income from renting out the others. This can be achieved by bringing in roommates, who share common spaces with you, or buying a multi-unit property like a duplex and renting out the other unit(s). The rent from your tenants can help offset your living expenses and, in some cases, may even bring you a monthly profit (meaning that you're living for free).

Mortgage: A loan to buy a house; the house itself serves as collateral for the loan. This means, if you fail to make your loan payments, the bank that issued your mortgage could potentially take ownership of your home.

Down Payment: The initial cash lump sum you need to pay when buying a house. "Standard" down payments equal 20% of a home's purchase price, though first-time homebuyers can put as little as 3.5% down if they qualify for an FHA loan.

Closing Costs: Fees and expenses that must be paid to the different parties in a real estate transaction when buying a home. Closing costs can include lender fees, appraisal costs, title insurance, and real estate agent fees.

Pre-approval: The process of being approved for a mortgage before you've found a house to buy. Your lender will evaluate your financial situation and approve you for a loan up to a certain amount. Getting pre-approved gives you a clear picture of what price range of homes you should consider and strengthens your position as a serious buyer.

Ingredient List

Required:

- Financial stability (ensure you can bear the costs of owning the property, even if you don't have renters)
- Willingness to live with roommates and/or manage tenants
- Emergency fund (to deal with unexpected property costs)

Recipe

Note: This recipe assumes that you don't currently own a property, but want to buy one with the intention of house hacking it.

1. Educate yourself and confirm that house hacking is a path you want to take. Are you willing to become a landlord?
2. Define your goals for house hacking. Do you just want a room-mate to help offset your mortgage? Or do you want to generate a net profit from house hacking? This will determine what type of property you buy.
3. Get pre-approved for a mortgage. Reach out to several different mortgage lenders in your area, and request pre-approval for a mortgage. Having a multitude of options will often lead to receiving more favorable interest rates on your loan (many offer price matching if you find a loan with a lower interest rate). At this step, you can also discuss your different loan and down payment options with your lender. Lower down payment loans may make it easier for you to buy a property, but they'll come with larger monthly payments, which makes it more difficult to profit month-to-month from house hacking. Getting pre-approved doesn't cost you anything: The mortgage lender only gets paid if you buy a home with their loan.
4. Interview a handful of real estate agents that specialize in working with house hackers. They'll have intimate knowledge of the market, which properties will and won't work for house hacking, know the ins and outs of negotiating, and may even have access to off-market deals. Like mortgage lenders, they don't get paid unless you buy a home through them.
5. Start your home search. Depending on your loan options and goals with house hacking, you could look at properties ranging from single-family homes to quadplexes.
6. When you find a property that fits your criteria, make an offer on it and go through the closing process (see Section 7.3 for a more detailed explanation of this process).

7. Renovate the property (if needed). If you're getting a good deal on a property, you'll likely need to put some work into it to make it an appealing place to rent for potential tenants. If you plan on furnishing your rental units, also do that during this step.

8. Find tenants. Post a listing for your unit(s) or room(s) on a website like Zillow or Apartments.com. Ensure you include high-quality pictures of your property (ideally taken by a professional photographer), and make sure the rent you're asking for is in line with the other properties in your area. If it's not, it could lead your property to sit vacant for an extended period of time, which will cost you more money than lowering your rent would've in the first place.

9. Properly screen potential tenants. Aside from a plumbing malfunction or storm damage, most of the horror stories you hear from real estate investors come from bad tenants. Require them to undergo a background check, ask for references from prior landlords, and verify their financial stability (employment). This person could potentially be living in your property for the next couple of years; you want to do everything in your power to ensure they don't make your life harder than it needs to be.

10. Select your tenant(s), ensure you have them sign a legally binding rental agreement, and collect a security deposit (typically equal to one month's rent).

11. Manage the property. As the landlord, you're responsible for promptly addressing maintenance requests, making improvements to the property, and meeting the needs of your tenants. It's also wise to enroll your tenants in an autopay program for their rent, so you don't need to worry about them missing payments and you can avoid dealing with physical checks.

12. Monitor, adjust, and expand. Consistently review your house hacking strategy to ensure the numbers still align with your goals, monitor the rental market to ensure your rents match market rates, and consider refinancing your mortgage if interest rates drop significantly. If you like this whole house hacking thing, consider investing in more real estate.

Recap

1. Clearly define your goals for house hacking.
2. Get pre-approved for a mortgage with multiple lenders.
3. Interview and select a real estate agent who specializes in working with house hackers (or real estate investors in general).
4. Find and close on a property that meets your criteria.
5. Post a listing for your property that utilizes professional photography and aligns with market rents.
6. Heavily screen potential tenants to minimize the risk of potential headaches for you. Choose the most qualified tenants, have them sign a legally binding rental agreement, and collect a security deposit from them.
7. Do your job as a landlord: handle the maintenance and improvements on the property, and meet the needs of your tenants.
8. Continue to monitor and adjust your strategy (if needed). If you like real estate investing, consider investing in more properties.

Chapter 8
How to Make More Money

8.1 How to Negotiate Your Starting Salary and Signing Bonus

Setup Time	Maintenance Time	Function
1 Hour	N/A	Make Money

Negotiating your starting pay may have the largest impact of any action in this book. Why? Assuming you stay on the same career path your entire adult life, your starting salary is the basis (in one way or another) of every raise you receive afterward. This recipe will take you through the process I personally used to raise my starting salary by $15,000 at my first job out of college.

Essential Terminology

Starting Salary: The initial base salary offered by your employer in a formal job offer. Assuming you receive raises as a percentage (for example, a 2%, 5%, or 10% raise) of your salary, this number is the foundation of all your future income in this career path.

Signing Bonus: A one-time payment provided by an employer as an incentive to accept a job offer. It typically comes with certain stipulations, like requiring that you stay with the company for a specified amount of time, to keep the full bonus.

Ingredient List

Required:

- At least one job offer
- Research on salary ranges
- Willingness to negotiate

Optional:

- Multiple job offers (highly recommended)

Recipe

1. Before you do anything, research the salary range you should expect to make in the role you're applying for. This can vary based on many factors, like experience and location, but it's good to have a baseline understanding of what to expect.

   a. Bonus points if you can find market research backing up these salary ranges. When I graduated college, my business school put together a report detailing the average starting salaries for each major. I downloaded this report and used it in my salary negotiations to provide another data point for why I should be paid more.

2. Apply to multiple jobs. This is required to get an offer in the first place, but the real power comes when you have multiple job offers for the same type of position.

3. Once you receive an offer, initiate negotiations via email (this tends to be the easiest). If you receive your offer verbally over the phone, request that they also send it to you via email and inform them that you'll need some time to read it over and compare it against your other offers (if you have any).

4. Speaking of other offers. That's the best way to begin a negotiation (again, if you have any). Though many different factors go into the total compensation you receive, I believe base salary to be the most important of all of them because it's what all of your future raises will be based on: The higher your starting salary, the higher your next raise will be, and the higher the raise

after that will be, and so on. So, if a competing offer has a higher base salary, make this clear to all companies that provided lower offers. You don't need to name the competitor, but you can say something like:

a. "I'm excited at the potential to work at (Company A), but, to be completely transparent, I've received an offer from (Company B) that comes with a base salary that is $10,000 higher than what you offered. Are you able to match this salary?"

b. This is how I turned my original $50,000 base salary offer at my first job (we'll call it Company A) into a starting salary of $65,000. All I did was apply to another job that had a $60,000 starting salary, tell the manager at Company A that I did so, and Company A immediately increased their offer to that $65,000 starting salary. All I had to do to bump my starting salary up $15,000 was send a couple emails, though it's important to note why Company A was willing to increase the offer so much to keep me: I was able to prove my value to them through a 3-month-long internship before receiving a full-time offer.

5. Bring the signing bonus into play (if there is one). Signing bonuses are great, but don't let them distract you from a low salary. Employers may purposefully offer an attractive signing bonus to "make up for" a lower-than-market salary, though what they're actually doing is ensuring they pay you less over your career (assuming you stay with them for the long term). Signing bonuses aren't used to determine your future raises; your base salary is. Because of this, if your potential employer refuses to budge on salary, it can be a smart long-term move to offer a "concession" of a lower signing bonus in exchange for a higher base salary. Some companies may not be willing or able to play ball here, but others will be.

6. Throw the rest of your negotiating toolkit at them. This could include:

a. Your unique skills and experiences (including past internships)

b. Market research for the salary range of the position you're applying for

7. Be responsive during the negotiation process, and realize that it could take some time. If any of the offers you received come with hard deadlines, do your best to make this the hard deadline of all your negotiations. This will encourage your prospective employers to give you a final answer before you lose out on a potential opportunity elsewhere.

8. Once you've received all final offers, grade them based on criteria such as:
   a. Whether you actually think you'll enjoy the job
   b. Base salary
   c. Signing bonus
   d. Equity (stock) compensation
   e. Healthcare
   f. Location
   g. The team you'll work with
   h. The long-term prospects of the company (especially important if you'll receive stock)

9. Accept your offer, and get used to negotiating: You'll need to do it every year or two when raises come due and when you receive promotions or switch companies.

Recap

1. Research the salary range you can expect for the roles you're applying for.
2. Apply for multiple jobs: This will give you the most leverage during negotiations because you can pit the offers against each other.
3. Focus negotiations on increasing your base salary, as this will determine all your future raises in this role.
4. Offer to lower your signing bonus in exchange for an increased base salary, if it makes sense.
5. Ensure you sell yourself on your unique skills and experiences (including past internships), and, if possible, provide market research for the salary range of the position you're applying to.
6. Compare offers and accept the one that is most appealing to you.
7. Prepare to negotiate during your future raises and negotiations.

8.2   How to Ask for a Raise

Setup Time	Maintenance Time	Function
1 Hour	N/A	Make Money

No matter who you are or what job you have, chances are, you feel like you're overworked and underpaid. In order to remedy this (at least for a short while), this recipe will teach you how to effectively ask your boss for a raise.

Essential Terminology

Raise: An increase in the salary or hourly pay for an employee, typically either to adjust for inflation or in recognition of the value provided to the workplace.

Ingredient list

Required:

- Do work throughout the year that is worth receiving the raise

Recipe

1. Make an effort each week throughout the year to go above and beyond and provide truly valuable work for your company. If you provide consistent results, it'll be hard to argue against you deserving a bump in pay.
2. While you're doing this outstanding work, clearly document your results. Whether this is cost savings, customers acquired, or patents filed, you want to have hard numbers to present to your boss when it's eventually time to request a raise.
3. Based on the value you provide, and based on the compensation of either your coworkers or other companies that are hiring for similar roles, come up with a solid number that you have in mind for your pay increase.

4. After you've done a minimum of six months to one year of this excellent work, request a meeting with your supervisor to discuss your compensation. It's good practice to send them an email overview of your request, along with your results, prior to the meeting, and give them plenty of time to look it over. You don't want to hide the intentions of the meeting, as your boss will likely need some time to analyze their department budget to determine how much can be allocated to your raise.

   a. If you provide legitimate value to your company, especially if you make a greater contribution than others in your same role, your boss will have a very easy case to make to their higher-ups about why you deserve a raise.

5. During your meeting, further present your case by diving deeper into your results, and clearly ask for the raise that you're looking for. Address any questions or concerns your boss may have and, if a raise to your salary isn't currently an option, discuss other ways that you may be rewarded. This could include additional bonuses, benefits, promotions, or professional development opportunities.

6. Follow up after the meeting and tell your boss that you appreciate their time. Let them know you're around to answer any follow-up questions they may have and that you're looking forward to hearing back.

   a. If you're not happy with your boss's answer, you could always present your results to other companies actively hiring for your position on the open market. Who knows, your boss may (suddenly) be able to meet your raise request once he sees that you have an offer from a competitor in your hand.

Recap

1. Go above and beyond to drive tangible results for your business; this will make you valuable in the eyes of the company.

2. Clearly document the results you drive for the company during a six-month to a one-year period.
3. Come up with a number you'd like to request for your raise that is based on the value you provide to the company and what other high performers in your role are being paid.
4. Set up a meeting with your boss to discuss your compensation. Present a snippet of your argument in your email so your boss can thoroughly analyze your results and requested raise before your meeting.
5. Follow up after your meeting and, if you don't like their answer, you now have six months to one year of solid results you can use to apply for roles at other companies.

8.3 How to Maximize Your Employee Benefits

Setup Time	Maintenance Time	Function
30–60 Minutes	30 Minutes per Year	Make Money

How many times have you heard someone say "it's not about the salary, it's about the *benefits*"? Employee benefits are an important part of your overall compensation that you must ensure you're taking full advantage of. This recipe walks you through how to maximize the most common benefits provided to employees.

Essential Terminology

Employee Benefits: Non-wage compensation provided to employees. This could include health insurance, retirement plans, paid time off, life insurance, FSAs, HSAs, and employee stock purchase plans.

Health Insurance: An insurance plan provided to employees by their employer that helps cover medical expenses. The employer may pay all or part of the premiums; any premiums passed down to the employee can be paid on a pre-tax basis.

Employer-Sponsored Retirement Plan (often a 401(k)): A retirement plan offered to employees by their employer that allows them to contribute a percentage of their salary to a tax-advantaged investment account. Employers may also provide matching contributions, where they contribute additional money into an employee's retirement account if the employee is also contributing money to their retirement account.

Employer Stock Purchase Plan (ESPP): A program offered by an employer that allows employees to purchase company stock at a discounted price.

Flexible Spending Account (FSA): An account that lets employees set aside money, tax free, to pay for eligible medical expenses. A portion of the money inside of an FSA is "use it or lose it": You can only carry forward a small amount to the following year.

Health Savings Account (HSA): A tax-advantaged investing (yes, you can invest in it despite its name) account available to those covered by a high-deductible health plan. Like a traditional IRA, the money you contribute to your HSA is tax-deductible, the funds inside the account grow tax free, and, the unique part of HSAs: Money withdrawn from the account to pay for qualified medical expenses is also tax free. When you reach age 65, the ability to withdraw your funds tax free to pay for medical expenses remains, but you also unlock the ability to withdraw your funds for any purposes without penalty (though you are taxed on them).

401(k) Match: The amount of money your employer contributes to your 401(k). Yeah, you heard that right: Employers often incentivize their employees to contribute to their 401(k)s by "matching" the contributions made by an employee up to a certain limit.

Ingredient List

Required:

- A job that offers employee benefits
- Knowledge of your employee benefits offerings
- Understanding of the eligibility criteria and enrollment periods

Recipe

1. Review your benefits package. When joining a new company, you'll be bombarded with pamphlets and booklets detailing all your various employee benefits. It's easy to get overwhelmed, but taking the time up front to review and understand these policies is essential to taking full advantage of your benefits.
2. Start by evaluating retirement benefits. If your employer offers a retirement plan (like a 401(k); see Section 2.3), contribute at least enough money to qualify for the maximum employer match (if any). For example: if your employer matches your contributions to your 401(k) dollar-for-dollar up to 5% of your total salary, you better elect for at least a 5% contribution to your 401(k). This match is essentially free money, plus you'll get the tax-saving benefits of contributing to a plan like a 401(k).
3. Optimize your health insurance coverage. This is discussed in-depth in Section 12.2, but it's important to thoroughly analyze the coverage options and whether you can get access to an FSA or HSA (see Section 12.1 for more information on HSAs).
4. See if your company offers an Employee Stock Purchase Plan (ESPP). ESPPs allow you to buy company stock at a discounted price via payroll deductions, allowing you to benefit even more from future increases in the company's stock price. Even if you aren't a huge believer in your company's long-term growth prospects, you can generally sell stock purchased through an ESPP at any time. Since you buy it for a discount (though this could lag

real-time market prices), there's a good chance that you could sell it for a profit right away.

5. Remember to use your paid time off (PTO). In recent years, it has become a lot more popular to offer employees "unlimited" PTO instead of the standard two to four weeks of allotted PTO per year. On the surface, this may sound like a good thing, but in more aggressive work environments, it becomes a lot easier to get shamed into not using PTO when you don't have a set amount to burn by the end of the year.

6. Explore additional benefits. Your employer may offer a whole slew of additional benefits, including life insurance, disability insurance, commuter benefits, wellness programs, pet insurance, immigration assistance, student loan assistance, continuing education assistance, mentorship programs, employee discounts, and many more.

7. Attend employee benefits workshops. Yes, this may sound like the most boring thing in the world, but setting aside 30 minutes to an hour of your time once a year to ensure you're fully utilizing all the benefits you want to be using is worth it in the grand scheme of things.

8. Review and update your elections as needed. If you go through major life events, like getting married, having children, or even just getting a raise, you may want to revisit the benefits you've enrolled in.

Recap

1. Thoroughly review your benefits package so you're aware of all the major, and minor, benefits you get access to from your employer.
2. Evaluate your retirement benefits, and, if there's an employer match, elect to contribute enough to your retirement plan to max out the match.
3. Evaluate your health insurance coverage options. See if any offer FSAs or HSAs.

4. See if your employer offers stock-based compensation programs, like ESPP.
5. *Please* remember to use your PTO, especially if your company has implemented an "unlimited" PTO policy.
6. Explore additional benefits offered by your employer.
7. Review and update your elections as needed.

8.4   How to Raise Your Salary by Job-Hopping without Ruining Your Reputation

Setup Time	Maintenance Time	Function
Many Years	N/A	Make Money

The best way to maximize your income is to stay loyal to one company for your entire career and consistently perform good work, right? Right? According to the Federal Reserve Bank of Atlanta, that's not how things work in reality: Since 1997 (when the first data set is available), those who switch jobs nearly always benefit from higher wage growth than those who stay put (https://www .atlantafed.org/chcs/wage-growth-tracker.aspx?panel=1). In April 2023, the average job switcher received wage growth of 7.6%, while the average job stayer only received a 5.6% raise (https://www .atlantafed.org/chcs/wage-growth-tracker.aspx?panel=1). It turns out, it can *pay* to change jobs. This recipe will teach you how to maximize your pay with job hopping, while still keeping your professional reputation intact.

Essential Terminology

Job Hopping: The practice of changing jobs frequently to pursue better opportunities, higher salaries, or career growth.

Ingredient List

Required:

- Clear career goals and objectives
- Strong negotiating skills
- Strong networking skills
- Strong work ethic

Recipe

1. As hard as it may be when you're just starting out, define your career goals as clearly as possible. How much money do you want to make, what role do you want to have, and what projects do you want to work on? Work backward from this ideal career to determine the path you need to take to get there.
2. If you don't already have a job, choose to start with a company where you can truly see yourself staying for a long time. This seems counterintuitive, but the ideal situation is that your current employer pays you what you're worth and offers ample growth opportunities. Sadly, this is rarely the case.
3. While working this first job, do everything you can to drive tangible results. Whether this is sales, page views, meetings booked (whatever), just have tangible results that you can eventually present to your boss (and other companies).
4. Build a strong network with other people in your industry. Attend conferences and meetups to, well, meet other people in your niche. You never know where your next opportunity will come from and, if you do make job hopping a habit, someone who personally knows you would be less likely to see that as a red flag on your resume when thinking about hiring you.
5. As you work, continue to build your skills and knowledge. If it's common for people in your career path to acquire professional certifications, do that as well. This will continue to build your value in the working world.
6. Here's the moment of truth: It's time to ask for a raise and/or promotion from your current boss (see Section 8.2 for details on how to effectively do this), but, before you do, apply to a

handful of other jobs that offer the amount of career and salary advancement you're looking for. You'll be an easy sell to them if you drove the results we talked about in Step 3. Assuming you do earn an offer or two from external companies, your current boss will have a choice to make during your compensation meeting: Do they match the other offers to keep you happy and retain a key player on their team, or will they let you walk? For some reason that makes no sense to me, corporations don't tend to value the employees they currently have and would rather let them walk than pay them what the market says they're worth. If that's the case with your employer, it may be time to job-hop.

   a. However, while switching companies, it's important to keep everything as cordial as possible. Future employers often ask for references from old managers and coworkers, so you want to make it clear to them that the only reason you're leaving is because you were offered a better opportunity elsewhere that you gave them a chance to match.

7. Repeat this cycle every couple of years when you feel ready for advancement but your current company isn't giving it to you. However, you should wait a minimum of two years before leaving a company (unless a *really* good offer comes across your desk), as leaving a company before then can be seen as a lack of commitment. Also, changing jobs every two years like clockwork doesn't look good either (how would you feel as an employer looking at a prospective employee's resume and seeing that they only stay at companies for two years?). Only change companies when you're offered a tangibly better opportunity, as this will be easier to explain in future interviews. Just be aware that, if you have a history of job hopping, this will be something prospective employers want to discuss during your interviews.

Recap

1. Clearly define your career goals; this allows you to work backward to achieve them.
2. Do everything you can to add value to your current workplace and your skills.

3. When you feel ready for advancement in your career, send out a couple of applications for job listings that seem ideal for you and schedule a meeting with your manager to discuss your role and compensation. Ideally, you'll receive a couple of offers from external companies, and this will give your manager the choice of matching their offers or letting you walk.

4. If you're serious about career advancement, you'll likely walk to the better offer. Keep everything cordial with your former employer; let them know you only left because you received a tangibly better offer for your career and that you gave them a chance to match.

5. Repeat this process every couple of years when you feel ready for career advancement, but make sure you don't overdo it as it can be a huge red flag for potential employers if you switch jobs every year or two.

8.5   How to Start a Side Hustle

Setup Time	Maintenance Time	Function
30–60 Minutes	Various	Make Money

Starting a side hustle was the best decision I've made for my career. Back in August of 2020, I posted my very first video on a brand-new TikTok page called "@nicktalksmoney." I thought it'd be a fun little side hustle to fill my time during lockdowns, and my initial goal (which felt crazy at the time) was to eventually bring in $1,000 or $2,000 per month in income from it. Just over a year later, in December of 2021, I was consistently making twice as much income from my social media accounts as I was from my day job, so I decided to take my side hustle full-time, and business has only gotten better since. You never know what a side hustle (especially one that's built around your passion) will turn into, and hey, if it "only" brings in a couple hundred or a couple thousand dollars per month, that's still a win! This recipe will teach you how to effectively start a side hustle, along with all the nitty-gritty business setup details you need to know.

Essential Terminology

Side Hustle: A flexible job or business that you work on in your free time to bring in additional income. Side hustles can range from gig economy work and freelancing, where you're trading your time directly for money, to starting and scaling a business, as I did with my social media accounts.

Ingredient List

Required:

- Computer or smartphone
- Willingness to give up some of your free time every week
- Business licenses (depending on your side hustle)

Optional:

- Entrepreneurial mindset
- Marketable skills or knowledge

Recipe

1. Determine whether you want to make some money immediately, or put in more time building a business (which may not make money for a while) that could potentially make you a lot more money down the line.
   a. If you want to make extra money to cover your bills, starting a side hustle in the gig economy (like ride sharing or food delivery) is the surefire way to get paid (around) a set amount for each hour you side hustle.

b. If you already have a stable job that pays the bills, but have always wanted to pursue a passion project, starting a side hustle based on your unique skills or knowledge may be the best path for you.

Note: Because the process of side hustling in the gig economy is fairly straightforward, the rest of the recipe will focus on side hustling to build a business and side hustling as a freelancer.

2. Research market demand. If you have a unique passion, skill-set, or knowledge base that you want to share with the world, ensure the world actually has demand for it. Search the internet for other people or businesses doing what you want to do, and if it looks like they are having success, it probably means there's space for you in the market as well (as long as you properly differentiate your services).

   a. When starting my side hustle, I knew that there were three things that people have been interested in since the dawn of civilization: health, wealth, and relationships. Since I had a unique knowledge base of the wealth space, I was pretty confident that somebody, somewhere would be interested in listening to me talk about money. However, I wanted to be sure that people on TikTok specifically (it was the hottest social media app at the time) didn't just want to watch videos of people dancing and driving trucks through the mud, but that they were interested in learning about money as well. So I downloaded the TikTok app and searched "personal finance": To my delight, there were half a dozen or so accounts with substantial followings that created personal finance content. This validated that the market had an interest in what I was thinking about offering, which gave me the confidence I needed to get started.

3. Create a business plan or roadmap for your side hustle. In this business plan, you need to answer three key questions: 1) What product or service will I offer? 2) How will I get attention for

my product or service? 3) How will I effectively monetize my product or service?

a. My initial business plan was pretty basic, but it got the job done. This is how I answered those three questions:

   i. **Answer 1:** I give away personal finance knowledge for free, which builds trust with my audience, which will then allow me to profit from affiliate links and brand sponsorships for products I truly believe will be beneficial for my viewers.

   ii. **Answer 2:** In the social media business, getting your first viewers and building a meaningful following are the hardest hurdles you'll face. I was very intentional about choosing TikTok as my starting platform. At the time, its algorithm was the only one that guaranteed your first handful of videos would be seen by a couple hundred people. Even if you were a brand-new account with zero followers, TikTok would show your videos to a couple hundred people on their "For You Page," and if the video performed well with that initial batch of viewers, it'd get pushed out to more people, and so on until video performance ultimately dropped. On all the other major social platforms at the time, if you started with zero followers, you'd be lucky to get three views on a post. The lesson here: Choose a platform that is incentivized in helping your side hustle succeed if it provides true value to the users of the platform.

   iii. **Answer 3:** As I mentioned in answer 1 above, my major goal was to build an audience large enough to bring in revenue from brand deals and affiliate offers. I came to this conclusion because that's how the "finance influencers" that came before me on YouTube built six- and seven-figure businesses for themselves. If that model worked for them on YouTube, why wouldn't it work for me on TikTok?

4. Before you start: If you have a full-time job, inform your boss about your plan to start a side hustle and ask for their approval. In most instances, you'll be fine, but you want to protect yourself from a situation where your boss finds out about your "secret" side hustle, isn't happy with it, and forces you to choose between your job or your side hustle, or potentially worse.

5. The hardest part: actually getting started and staying consistent with it. Start by dedicating an hour or two every Saturday morning, and ramp up your time commitment as you're able to. Build your brand, hone in on your offerings, and start marketing.

6. Don't be afraid to fail, as long as you overdeliver on the fix. In *any* business, there will be a time when the business lets the customer down. If you can aggressively and immediately offer a high-value fix for your customer, that's an experience they'll always remember and share with their circle.

   a. Imagine if you went to a restaurant, and the waiter forgot to tell the kitchen to make the side dish you ordered. If, when you told the waiter about this, they not only corrected the baseline issue by bringing you the side dish but also brought out a bottle of champagne and gave you a gift card to use the next time you visit the restaurant, would you still be upset that they originally missed your side dish order? No way! You'd be impressed at the world-class service they provided for you.

7. Side hustle bookkeeping: especially when you're just starting out, this doesn't have to be anything fancy. Keep a spreadsheet that details all your income and expenses, and get a business credit card that you only use for side hustle–related expenses. When filing your taxes, you'll likely just report everything on your Schedule C as a sole proprietor (see Section 9.2). However, if you have a business partner or a more complex operation, it would be worth consulting an accountant or business attorney to learn how to properly structure your business entity.

8. Know when to take your side hustle full-time. Sometimes side hustles stay side hustles forever, and that's great! But if your side

hustle has the potential to turn into something bigger, here are three signs that you should take the leap into becoming a full-time business owner:

a. Your side hustle is already bringing in enough income for you to sustain yourself off of it if needed. I set an overly-cautious goal of wanting to make double the salary of my day job from my side hustle for three months in a row before I considered taking it full-time. Looking back on it, because of the next two reasons on this list, I should've made the jump a lot sooner.

b. You have an emergency fund (Section 1.3) large enough to sustain your lifestyle for at least six to twelve months. This, along with the income you're making from your side hustle, should give you plenty of runway to try to make this thing work. An emergency fund helps you avoid the stress of counting on the money coming in per month from your side hustle to cover rent and groceries.

c. It's clear that if you had more time to dedicate to your side hustle, you'd make more money. For me, if I could put a full week's worth of work into my content creation business, I'd be able to make more videos, which would lead to more followers, which would lead to larger sponsorship deals. I'd also be able to dedicate time to other projects like starting an email newsletter, putting together educational courses, making long-form YouTube videos, and even writing a book! This turned out to be the right decision for me because my side hustle income increased more than 500% the year after I made it my main hustle.

Recap

1. Decide whether you want a side hustle where you strictly trade time for money, or whether you want to try to build a business.
2. If it's the latter, find the intersection of your passion and what people are actually willing to pay you for.

3. Create a business plan.
4. If you have a full-time job, ask your employer for explicit permission to pursue a side hustle during non-working hours.
5. Get started, and dedicate a set amount of time each week to work on your side hustle to ensure you make progress.
6. Over-fix any mistakes you make while serving customers.
7. Get a business credit card that you only use on side hustle expenses, and keep a spreadsheet with all your income and expenses listed on it for each year.
8. You'll know it's time to take your side hustle full-time when it's generating enough income for you to live comfortably, you have an emergency fund of 6 to 12 months to cover you in case you hit some speed bumps, and it's clear that putting more time into your side hustle will lead to more income.

Chapter 9
Taxes

9.1 How to Pay Taxes If You Have a Normal Job

Setup Time	Maintenance Time	Function
30 Minutes–2 Hours	N/A	Paying Taxes

As the old saying goes, there are only two certainties in life: death and taxes. Since taxes are the primary source of revenue for the US government, you'd think they'd make sure schools would at least go over the basics of how to pay them. Well, they don't, so this recipe will walk you through how to pay taxes if you have a "normal" job. (If you're a business owner, independent contractor, or freelancer, see Section 9.2 for that.)

Essential Terminology

IRS: The Internal Revenue Service. This is the governmental agency in charge of taxation.
Tax Return: The aggregation of the tax forms you fill out, which tells the government how much you made in a year, how much tax you already paid through withholdings, and how much you owe or are due as a refund.

Tax Withholdings: Money deducted from your paychecks and paid to the tax authorities to help satisfy your tax liability for the year. Withholdings are why your paychecks are never as big as you think they'd be.

Form W-4: A form provided to your employer that tells them how much tax to withhold from your paychecks. You fill one out right when you get a new job, and you can submit a revised version whenever you want to update your withholding amounts. Reasons to submit a new Form W-4 include a change in marital status, an increase in the number of dependents (usually kids, sometimes older parents), and other tax credits or deductions.

IRS Free File Program: A partnership between the IRS and select tax software companies that lets you file your taxes for free, as long as your income is below a certain level. For the 2022 tax filing season, taxpayers must've had an adjusted gross income of less than $73,000 to qualify for the free-file program. Using the IRS free file doesn't mean that you won't owe taxes; it means you don't have to pay a tax software provider or accountant to file your taxes for you. Find a list of IRS free file providers at: https://apps.irs.gov/app/freeFile/.

Form W-2: A tax form that details your income and withholdings as an employee. If you are a full-time or part-time employee, you'll be issued a Form W-2 by your employer shortly after the end of each year.

Tax Filing Deadline: The "standard" deadline to file your tax return for the previous year is April 15th of the following year. For example, on your tax return that was due in April 2023, you would've reported all of your income, withholdings, and other taxable items from 2022. The April 15th deadline will be pushed back to the next business day if it falls on a weekend or holiday (if April 15th fell on a Saturday, taxes would be due that following Monday, April 17th).

Tax Liability: The payment you must make to the IRS when filing your tax return if you didn't withhold enough taxes from your paychecks throughout the year.

Tax Refund: The payment you receive from the IRS when filing your tax return if you withheld too much from your paychecks throughout the year.

De Minimis: If a tax form says "De Minimis" on it, you don't need to file that tax form. This often applies to Form 1099-INTs issued by checking accounts, as the interest paid to you by that checking account is too small to make a material impact on your tax return.

Ingredient List

Required:

- Computer (smartphone could work but not recommended)
- Social Security number or ITIN
- Bank account information (for direct deposit or withdrawal of your tax liability or refund)

Optional:

- Tax filing software (can be free with IRS Free File)
- Accountant

Recipe

1. Understand when taxes are due and how they're paid. The "standard" deadline to file your tax return for the previous year is April 15th of the following year. For example, on your tax return that was due in April 2023, you would've reported all of your income, withholdings, and other taxable items from 2022. Your tax return tells the IRS how much money you made, how much you withheld, and either how much more you owe them or how large of a refund they owe you.

2. When you start a part- or full-time job, you'll need to fill out a Form W-4. This determines the amount of taxes withheld from your paychecks. There is a worksheet included on the W-4 you can fill out to determine what is likely a fine withholding amount for you, though you can always update it later by submitting another Form W-4.

3. From January to March every year, you'll receive most (if not all) of the tax documents you need to file your tax return. These documents should either be mailed or emailed to you, but sometimes you may need to log in to the website of something like

your bank or broker to download your tax forms. Here's a list of common tax documents and who they may be issued by:

a. Form W-2: reports your employment income and withholdings, issued to you by your employer(s).

b. Form 1099-INT: reports interest earned, typically in a bank account, high-yield savings account (HYSA), or brokerage account.

c. Form 1099-DIV: reports dividends earned, typically issued to you by your brokerage account.

d. Form 1099-B: reports capital gains and losses, typically issued to you by your brokerage account.

e. Consolidated 1099: combines your 1099-INT, 1099-DIV, and 1099-B from your brokerage account.

f. Form 1099-MISC: reports any miscellaneous income you earned over $600 from a single person or entity during the year.

g. Form 1098: a statement detailing your mortgage interest paid (which can be a deductible expense), issued to you from the bank where you hold your mortgage.

h. Form 1098-T: details the amount you paid for college tuition (which can be a deductible expense), issued to you by your college/university.

4. Don't intentionally misreport any information on your tax return. Not only are *you* sent a copy of your tax documents, but *the IRS* is as well, so they'll know if anything is off and slap you with some potentially serious penalties like fines and jail time.

5. Decide how to file your tax return; here are the three main methods:

a. If you qualify for the IRS Free File program, use one of the tax software providers listed here (https://apps.irs.gov/app/freeFile) to file your taxes for free.

b. If you don't qualify for the IRS Free File program, you could pay a fee (usually a couple hundred dollars) to file taxes through one of the major tax software providers.

c. If you want to be as hands-off with the tax filing process as possible and are ok spending a little bit more for professional help, hire an accountant to prepare and file your tax returns.

6. When your return has been prepared, review it in detail before you file to ensure everything is reported correctly. Pro tip: If you filed a tax return last year, compare the two documents to see if there are any areas you missed. For example, if you're about to file your 2022 tax return, but you see on your 2021 tax return that you reported dividend income from your brokerage account, you may realize that you forgot to include the information from your 2022 1099-DIV on your 2022 tax return.

7. One more step before you file: Ensure you're aware of whether you owe more money or are due a refund. Tax refunds are typically paid to you within a couple of days (sometimes a couple of weeks), while amounts due aren't required to be paid until the tax filing deadline. This means that, as long as you have all your tax documents, filing your tax return early won't hurt you—it'll only let you get your refund (if any) sooner.

8. Finally: File your tax return. This will send your tax return to the federal and state (if any, some states don't charge income taxes) tax authorities.

9. If the tax authorities have any questions (or see anything suspicious on your tax return), they'll mail you a letter asking for clarifying information.

Recap

1. Understand the general concept of filing taxes and when the tax filing deadline is.

2. When you start a job, fill out a Form W-4 to set your withholdings.

3. From January to March every year, collect your tax documents. Note that most (if not all) of these documents are *also* sent to the IRS, so don't try to omit any information on your tax return.

4. Decide how to file your taxes. The IRS Free File program is a great option for those who are under its income limit.

5. When your tax return has been prepared, compare it with your prior year's tax return to see if there's anything that's obviously missing.

6. File your tax return. If you owe the IRS more money, that's due by the tax filing deadline. If you're owed a refund, that'll be paid

out to you within a couple of days, weeks, or maybe even months, depending on how the IRS is feeling.

7. Don't faint if you see a letter from the IRS in the mail: They may just be asking a question about your tax return.

9.2   How to Pay Taxes as a Business Owner, Independent Contractor, or Freelancer

Setup Time	Maintenance Time	Function
30 Minutes–2 Hours	30 Minutes per Month	Paying Taxes

What's the reward for taking the path less traveled and working for yourself? A more complicated tax season. Unlike employees (see Section 9.1), you aren't simply handed a Form W-2 that details the income and withholdings you made for the prior year: You have to keep track of that yourself. This recipe will walk you through you how to file your taxes as a small business owner, freelancer, or independent contractor.

Essential Terminology

IRS: The Internal Revenue Service. This is the governmental agency in charge of taxation.

Tax Return: The aggregation of the tax forms you fill out, which tells the government how much you made in a year, how much tax you already paid through withholdings, and how much you owe or are due as a refund.

Estimated Tax Payments: A method for self-employed individuals to pay their taxes in advance. These payments take the place of tax withholdings and are due 4 times throughout the year: April 15th, June 15th, September 15th, and January 15th (if these were estimated tax payments for 2022, the first three dates would all be in 2022, and the January 15th deadline would be in 2023, right before your 2022 tax return is filed). Failure to make estimated tax payments may result in monetary penalties when you file your tax return.

Profit and Loss Statement: Otherwise known as a "P and L," it lists all of your business income and expenses for a tax year. It's vital for business owners to keep one, as they must accurately report their income on their tax return, and can use their expenses to reduce their total taxable income.

Schedule C: A tax form used by self-employed individuals to report their business income and expenses. It's filed as part of your personal tax return.

Form W-9: A form you send to your clients (or whoever is paying you) that lists the tax information of your business. Your clients need this to issue you your tax documents.

EIN: Employer Identification Number, it's basically like a Social Security number for your business. Sole proprietors and independent contractors aren't typically required to obtain one.

Tax Withholdings: Money deducted from your paychecks and paid to the tax authorities to help satisfy your tax liability for the year. Withholdings are why your paychecks are never as big as you think they'd be.

IRS Free File Program: A partnership between the IRS and select tax software companies that lets you file your taxes for free, as long as your income is below a certain level. For the 2022 tax filing season, taxpayers must've had an adjusted gross income of less than $73,000 to qualify for free file. Using IRS free file doesn't mean that you won't owe taxes; it means you don't have to pay a tax software provider or accountant to file your taxes for you. Find a list of IRS free file providers at: https://apps.irs.gov/app/freeFile/.

Form W-2: A tax form that details your income and withholdings as an employee. If you are a full-time or part-time employee, you'll be issued a Form W-2 by your employer shortly after the end of each year.

Tax Filing Deadline: The "standard" deadline to file your tax return for the previous year is April 15th of the following year. For example, on your tax return that was due in April 2023, you would've reported all of your income, withholdings, and other taxable items from 2022. The April 15th deadline will be pushed back to the next business day if it falls on a weekend or holiday (if April 15th fell on a Saturday, taxes would be due that following Monday, April 17th).

Tax Liability: The payment you must make to the IRS when filing your tax return if you didn't withhold enough taxes from your paychecks throughout the year.

Tax Refund: The payment you receive from the IRS when filing your tax return if you withheld too much from your paychecks throughout the year.

De Minimis: If a tax form says "De Minimis" on it, you don't need to file that tax form. This often applies to Form 1099-INTs issued by checking accounts, as the interest paid to you by that checking account is too small to make a material impact on your tax return.

Ingredient List

Required:

- Computer (smartphone could work but not recommended)
- Social Security number or ITIN
- Bank account information (for direct deposit or withdrawal of your tax liability or refund)
- Profit and loss statement

Optional:

- Tax filing software (can be free with IRS Free File)
- Accountant
- An EIN

Recipe

Note:This recipe is intended for sole proprietors and single-member LLCs. If you have a multi-member LLC or file taxes as a corporation, seek the guidance of a professional accountant.

1. Manage your finances with tax season in mind. If you're self-employed, it can be easy to lose track of what's a business expense vs personal expense. To combat this, open a credit card

that is specifically used for business purchases, open a business bank account, and create a profit and loss statement that you update whenever a relevant transaction occurs.

   a. Note that miles driven for business purposes (like driving to job sites, or miles driven for a ride-sharing service) are a deductible business expense; ensure you keep track of them.

2. If you're working as an independent contractor for clients, submit a Form W-9 when you begin work with them to ensure they can properly issue you your tax documents.

3. Throughout the year, estimate and make quarterly tax payments. These are required since we self-employed folk don't have taxes automatically withdrawn from our income throughout the year. The IRS has a whole page detailing who is required to make them, and how you figure them, here: https://www .irs.gov/businesses/small-businesses-self-employed/estimated-taxes.

   a. Failing to make estimated tax payments may result in a monetary penalty when filing your tax return.

4. From January to March every year, you'll receive most (if not all) of the tax documents you need to file your tax return. These documents should either be mailed or emailed to you, but sometimes you may need to log in to the website of something like your bank or broker to download your tax forms. Here's a list of common tax documents and who they may be issued by:

   a. 1099-NEC: reports your income from nonemployee compensation (NEC); this will likely be your most common tax form as a self-employed individual. Expect to receive one from each of your clients who paid you over $600 during the tax year.

   b. Form 1099-INT: reports interest earned, typically in a bank account, high-yield savings account (HYSA), or brokerage account.

   c. Form 1099-DIV: reports dividends earned, typically issued to you by your brokerage account.

   d. Form 1099-B: reports capital gains and losses, typically issued to you by your brokerage account.

   e. Consolidated 1099: combines your 1099-INT, 1099-DIV, and 1099-B from your brokerage account.

f. Form 1099-MISC: reports any miscellaneous income you earned over $600 from a single person or entity during the year.

g. Form 1098: a statement detailing your mortgage interest paid (which can be a deductible expense), issued to you from the bank where you hold your mortgage.

h. Form 1098-T: details the amount you paid for college tuition (which can be a deductible expense), issued to you by your college/university.

5. Don't intentionally misreport any information on your tax return. Not only are *you* sent a copy of your tax documents, but *the IRS* is as well, so they'll know if anything is off and slap you with some potentially serious penalties like fines and jail time. An over-reporting of common business expenses is also likely to draw attention from the IRS.

6. Decide how to file your tax return; here are the three main methods:

a. If you qualify for the IRS Free File program, use one of the tax software providers listed here https://apps.irs.gov/app/freeFile to file your taxes for free.

b. If you don't qualify for the IRS Free File program, you could pay a fee (usually a couple hundred dollars) to file taxes through one of the major tax software providers.

c. If you want to be as hands-off with the tax filing process as possible and are ok spending a little bit more for professional help, hire an accountant to prepare and file your tax returns. This is an especially good option for business owners, as there are a multitude of things you can do to reduce your tax bill that you might not be aware of. Just be sure that you choose an accountant who primarily works with people in a similar position as you.

7. Complete your tax forms. As a self-employed person, you'll report your business income and expenses on your personal tax return (unless you have a more complex business entity). Your personal income is reported on Form 1040 (the main page of the tax return), while your business income and expenses are reported on Schedule C (another form in the tax return). Your net business income will be reported on Schedule C, and

flow to Form 1040. This sounds complicated, but (if you prepare your taxes on your own) your tax software provider should ensure this is a fairly straightforward process.

8. When your return has been prepared, review it in detail before you file to ensure everything is reported correctly. Pro tip: if you filed a tax return last year, compare the two documents to see if there are any areas you missed. For example, if you're about to file your 2022 tax return, but you see on your 2021 tax return that you reported dividend income from your brokerage account, you may realize that you forgot to include the information from your 2022 1099-DIV on your 2022 tax return.

9. One more step before you file: Ensure you're aware of whether you owe more money or are due a refund. Tax refunds are typically paid to you within a couple of days (sometimes a couple of weeks), while amounts due aren't required to be paid until the tax filing deadline. This means that, as long as you have all your tax documents, filing your tax return early won't hurt you: it'll only let you get your refund (if any) sooner.

10. Finally: file your tax return. This will send your tax return to the federal and state (if any, some states don't charge income taxes) tax authorities.

11. If the tax authorities have any questions (or see anything suspicious on your tax return), they'll mail you a letter asking for clarifying information.

Recap

1. Manage your business finances with tax season in mind: open a business bank account, a business credit card, and create a profit and loss statement.
2. Send W-9s to the clients you work for as an independent contractor.
3. Throughout the year, calculate and make quarterly estimated tax payments.
4. From January to March every year, collect your tax documents. Note that most (if not all) of these documents are *also* sent to the IRS, so don't try to omit any information on your tax return.

5. Decide how to file your taxes. If you have a profitable business, it may be worth it to seek professional help. An accountant that knows what he's doing could save you more in taxes than he charges you for working with him.

6. Report your business income and losses on Schedule C of your tax return.

7. When your tax return has been prepared, compare it with your prior year's tax return to see if there's anything that's obviously missing.

8. File your tax return. If you owe the IRS more money, that's due by the tax filing deadline. If you're owed a refund, that'll be paid out to you within a couple of days, weeks, or maybe even months, depending on how the IRS is feeling.

9. Don't faint if you see a letter from the IRS in the mail: they may just be asking a question about your tax return.

9.3 How Investments Are Taxed

Setup Time	Maintenance Time	Function
30 Minutes	N/A	Paying Taxes

If Chapter 2 inspired you to start investing, congratulations! Investments can surely be financially rewarding, but they also come with unique tax rules you need to be aware of. As with basically any activity that makes you money, the IRS wants their cut. This recipe will teach you how these taxes work and how to do everything in your power to legally avoid them.

Essential Terminology

IRS: The Internal Revenue Service. This is the governmental agency in charge of taxation.

Tax Return: The aggregation of the tax forms you fill out, which tells the government how much you made in a year, how much tax you already paid through withholdings, and how much you owe or are due as a refund.

Brokerage Account: A non-retirement account that allows you to invest in stocks, bonds, index funds, ETFs, mutual funds, certificates of deposit, etc. There are no contribution, withdrawal, or income limits. Unlike retirement accounts, brokerage accounts do not offer tax-saving incentives for the money you deposit into them. They are free to open and don't have any ongoing account fees (at most major brokers).

Broker: It's a fancy way to refer to the company that hosts your brokerage account. Just like you associate "banks" like Chase, Wells Fargo, and Bank of America with checking accounts, you can associate "brokers" like Fidelity, Vanguard, and Charles Schwab with brokerage accounts. Brokers are specifically licensed to facilitate transactions on the stock market, whereas most "regular" banks aren't.

Capital Gains: The profit you make from selling an investment, such as stocks or index funds. For example, if you bought a stock for $100 and later sold it for $150, your capital gain would be $50. This $50 capital gain is the only part of this transaction that's taxed (your $100 "cost basis" isn't taxed). Capital gains on assets held for one year or less ("short-term capital gains") are taxed at your ordinary income tax rates (up to 37%), while long-term capital gains (assets that were sold after more than one year of you holding them) are taxed at a much lower rate (15% for most people, 20% is the highest rate). Note that these rates are subject to change, but are current as of 2023.

Capital Losses: The opposite of capital gains. This is what happens if you sell a stock for less than you bought it for. Capital losses aren't entirely a bad thing, however, as they can be used to offset taxable capital gains. For example, if, in 2022, you had a $2,000 capital gain and a $1,500 capital loss, you'd only have to pay taxes on $500 of your capital gains.

Cost Basis: The original purchase price of your investment.

Dividends: Cash distributions you may receive as the owner of certain stocks or funds. Dividends can be reinvested into the stocks or funds that paid them but are subject to taxes regardless of what you do with them.

Taxable Accounts: Investment accounts with no special tax advantages, like a brokerage account.

Tax-Advantaged Accounts: Special investment accounts, generally geared toward retirement savings, that provide certain tax benefits, like tax-deferred or tax-free growth. Examples include IRAs and 401(k)s.

Ordinary Income Tax Rate: The tax rate applied to the earnings from your job.

Ingredient List

Required:

- Brokerage account (see Section 2.1)
- An understanding of investment types (see Section 2.5)
- Awareness of tax brackets and rates
- Knowledge of the tax filing process (see Section 9.1)

Recipe

1. Investment taxes are paid when you file your tax return. Unlike income from your paycheck that may be automatically withheld to pay for taxes, investment taxes aren't paid until you file your tax return. This means, if you have a significant amount of investment activity during the year, you should prepare yourself for a large tax bill when you file your tax return.

   a. One question I get all the time is whether taxes on dividends or stock sales are owed if you keep your money inside your brokerage account. The answer is yes: It doesn't matter what you do with these proceeds, as long as they occurred inside of a brokerage account (and not a tax-advantaged account), you'll owe tax on them.

2. Know what tax forms to look out for. You don't need to worry about summing up all your investment income at the end of the year: Your broker will do that for you and summarize everything

on your tax forms. Common tax forms for investment-related income include:

   a. Form 1099-INT: reports interest earned, typically in a bank account, high-yield savings account (HYSA), or brokerage account.

   b. Form 1099-DIV: reports dividends earned, typically issued to you by your brokerage account.

   c. Form 1099-B: reports capital gains and losses, typically issued to you by your brokerage account.

   d. Consolidated 1099: combines your 1099-INT, 1099-DIV, and 1099-B from your brokerage account.

3. Understand capital gains tax. When you sell an investment for more than you bought it for, you'll likely be subject to capital gains taxes on your net profit (sale price minus your cost basis). Short-term capital gains (from investments held one year or less) are typically taxed at a much higher rate than long-term capital gains (investments held for over one year before selling).

   a. The best way to avoid (or at least defer) capital gains taxes is to hold your assets for a very long time. Active traders are penalized in the world of investing.

   b. See current capital gains tax rates at: https://www.irs.gov/taxtopics/tc409.

4. Be prepared for dividend taxation. Dividends paid out inside of your brokerage account are taxed, no matter whether you reinvest them or withdraw them as cash. "Qualified" dividends are taxed at long-term capital gains tax rates, while "non-qualified" dividends are taxed at your ordinary income tax rates.

5. Be prepared for taxable interest. If you hold a large amount of cash inside of something like a high-yield savings account (HYSA), money market fund, certificates of deposit, or bonds, you'll likely be paid some form of taxable interest. Most of this interest is taxed at the same rates as your ordinary income.

6. Leverage tax-advantaged accounts. Any investment activity (capital gains, dividends, interest) that happens within accounts like Roth IRAs, Traditional IRAs, and 401(k)s isn't taxed until you either withdraw these funds in retirement, or, in the case of Roth IRAs, they simply aren't taxed at all. These accounts allow you to

defer, or even completely *avoid*, taxes, so it's in your best interest to take full advantage of them.

7. Stay in the loop about tax law changes. When changes to the tax code are discussed, chances are investment taxes are involved somehow.

Recap

1. Understand that investment taxes aren't paid as the income is earned: They're paid when you file your tax return.
2. It doesn't matter what you do with your investment income, it's always taxed. The exception is if the income was generated inside of a tax-advantaged account like an IRA or 401(k).
3. You aren't responsible for keeping track of all your investment earnings (at least inside of a brokerage account); your broker will summarize your profits and losses on your tax documents.
4. Capital gains taxes are generated when you sell an asset for more than you bought it for. Holding something for longer than a year before selling it will reduce the rate this capital gain is taxed at.
5. Dividends are taxed no matter whether you reinvest them or withdraw them as cash. Interest is also a taxable item you'll likely generate.
6. Using tax-advantaged accounts will allow you to defer, or even completely avoid, investment taxes.

9.4   How Tax Extensions Work and How to File Them

Setup Time	Maintenance Time	Function
30 Minutes	N/A	Tax Filing

What happens if you're the world's ultimate procrastinator and the tax filing deadline sneaks up on you out of nowhere? Or what if you don't have all the documents you need to file your tax return by the deadline? That's where tax extensions come in. This recipe will teach you how tax extensions work and explain how to file them.

Essential Terminology

Tax Extension: A formal request submitted to the IRS to extend the deadline for filing your tax return by roughly six months. The standard filing deadline for extended tax returns is the following October 15th, though, just like the standard tax filing deadline, this will be pushed back to the next business day if it falls on a weekend or holiday. If you are expected to owe taxes, you must still pay this estimated amount when filing a tax extension. If you are expected to receive a refund, you won't receive this refund until your final tax return is filed.

Form 4868: The "Application for Automatic Extension of Time to File U.S. Individual Income Tax Return." This is the form you submit to the IRS to request a tax extension. On it, you must list your name, address, Social Security number (and your spouse's, if applicable), an estimate of your tax liability, and how much you've already paid toward your tax liability (through withholdings, for example). Use that to calculate your balance due and submit a payment of that balance due (can be paid online). You don't need to explain why you're asking for an extension, and you'll only be contacted if your request is denied.

IRS: The Internal Revenue Service. This is the governmental agency in charge of taxation.

Tax Return: The aggregation of the tax forms you fill out, which tells the government how much you made in a year, how much tax you already paid through withholdings, and how much you owe or are due as a refund.

Tax Withholdings: Money deducted from your paychecks and paid to the tax authorities to help satisfy your tax liability for the year. Withholdings are why your paychecks are never as big as you think they'd be.

Tax Filing Deadline: The "standard" deadline to file your tax return for the previous year is April 15th of the following year.

For example, on your tax return that was due in April 2023, you would've reported all of your income, withholdings, and other taxable items from 2022. The April 15th deadline will be pushed back to the next business day if it falls on a weekend or holiday (if April 15th fell on a Saturday, taxes would be due that following Monday, April 17th).

Tax Liability: The payment you must make to the IRS when filing your tax return if you didn't withhold enough taxes from your paychecks throughout the year.

Tax Refund: The payment you receive from the IRS when filing your tax return if you withheld too much from your paychecks throughout the year.

Form K-1: A tax document used to report your share of the income, deductions, and credits from certain entities, like companies or private equity investments.

Amended Tax Return: If you need to correct errors or make changes to a previously filed tax return, you file an amended tax return using form 1040-X. You generally have three years from the original due date of your tax return (including extensions) to file an amended return if it results in you receiving a refund. However, there's no time limit if you're amending a tax return to report additional income (which may cause you to generate a tax liability that you may owe interest and penalties on).

Ingredient List

Required:

- Accountant or tax preparation software
- A tax return complete with all the information you have so far

Recipe

1. Determine whether you actually need to file a tax extension. The only major benefit of filing a tax extension is that it extends the time allotted for you to file your tax return without incurring late filing fees and penalties. If you're projected to owe a tax liability, it does *not* give you more time to make this payment. Along with filing your

tax extension, it's required that you pay an estimate of your total tax liability by the standard filing deadline. If you don't, you may be subject to penalties and interest on the unpaid amount. Alternatively, if you are expected to receive a refund, you won't receive this refund until your final tax return is filed.

   a. The most common reason for needing to file an extension is that you haven't received all of your tax documents yet. Some tax documents, like Form K-1s, can take many months to prepare, and issue "estimated K-1s" to allow you to estimate your tax liability when filing your tax extension. Late K-1s were the main reason I filed tax extensions for clients back when I was a tax preparer.

2. Understand the time period of the extension. Filing a tax extension will grant you a roughly six-month extension for filing your final tax return. This means your final tax return is due by October 15th, or the next following business day if it lands on a weekend or holiday.

   a. Just because you have six additional months to file, this doesn't mean you should take the full additional six months to file. As outlined in Step 1, there's no benefit to waiting to file your tax return: Any refund you may be owed will only be issued when your final tax return is filed, and, if you didn't fully pay your estimated tax liability when filing your extension, you could be accruing penalties and interest on the unpaid amount.

3. If you determine an extension is necessary, complete and file Form 4858 (ideally, with the help of a tax professional). This form can be completed and filed electronically through tax preparation software. On it, you must list your name, address, Social Security number (and your spouse's, if applicable), an estimate of your tax liability (this is where a tax professional can really help you), and how much you've already paid toward your tax liability (through withholdings, for example). Use that to calculate your balance due and submit a payment of that balance due (can be paid online). You don't need to explain why you're asking for an extension, and you'll only be contacted if your request is denied.

4. It's good practice to keep a record of all filings you make with the IRS, and tax extensions are no exception. If filed electronically,

save a PDF copy of the submission confirmation page. This will help you in the event that the IRS has any questions about whether you filed for an extension on time/at all.

5. Complete and submit your tax return as soon as possible. Remember, an extension grants you roughly six more months to file your final tax return, but there is no benefit in waiting. Gather all necessary documentation and information to accurately complete your tax return, and file by the extension deadline of October 15th (or the following business day) to avoid penalties and interest. If anything arises later that would require you to update the tax return, you can file an amended tax return

Recap

1. Assess your situation to see if you really need to file a tax extension, or whether you just want to procrastinate.
2. Understand the additional time the extension will grant you to file your final tax return, which is typically six months.
3. Complete and submit Form 4868, along with an estimated tax payment (if you're expected to owe a tax liability), to request a tax extension.
4. Keep a copy of the tax extension submission confirmation page in your records.
5. File your finalized tax return as soon as possible; there's no benefit in waiting until the extended filing deadline.

9.5   How Amended Tax Returns Work and How to File Them

Setup Time	Maintenance Time	Function
30–60 Minutes	N/A	Tax Filing

Sometimes, after you file your tax return, you might realize that you've made a mistake, or a "corrected" tax document is sent to you that varies greatly from the document you used on your tax return. If this happens to you, it's not the end of the world: just ensure you correct these errors and plug in the updated information by filing an amended tax return. This recipe will explain how amended tax returns work and walk you through how to file them.

Essential Terminology

Amended Tax Return: If you need to correct errors or make changes to a previously filed tax return, you file an amended tax return using form 1040-X. You generally have three years from the original due date of your tax return (including extensions, or two years from the date you paid the tax, if later) to file an amended return if it results in you receiving a refund. However, there's no time limit if you're amending a tax return to report additional income (which may cause you to generate a tax liability that you may owe interest and penalties on).

Form 1040-X: The form you complete and file to submit an amended tax return. On it, you must enter the original amount of the incorrect line item (income, deductions, etc.) reported on your tax return, list the correct amount for that line item, and list the net change.

IRS: The Internal Revenue Service. This is the governmental agency in charge of taxation.

Tax Return: The aggregation of the tax forms you fill out, which tells the government how much you made in a year, how much tax you already paid through withholdings, and how much you owe or are due as a refund.

Tax Withholdings: Money deducted from your paychecks and paid to the tax authorities to help satisfy your tax liability for the year. Withholdings are why your paychecks are never as big as you think they'd be.

Tax Filing Deadline: The "standard" deadline to file your tax return for the previous year is April 15th of the following year. For example, on your tax return that was due in April 2023, you would've reported all of your income, withholdings, and other taxable items from 2022. The April 15th deadline will be pushed back to the next business day if it falls on a weekend or holiday (if April 15th fell on a Saturday, taxes would be due that following Monday, April 17th).

Tax Liability: The payment you must make to the IRS when filing your tax return if you didn't withhold enough taxes from your paychecks throughout the year.

Tax Refund: The payment you receive from the IRS when filing your tax return if you withheld too much from your paychecks throughout the year.

Tax Extension: A formal request submitted to the IRS to extend the deadline for filing your tax return by roughly six months.

Corrected Tax Documents: If someone like your employer or bank sends you tax documents and realizes that they made a mistake on them (income, withholding, or similar numbers are reported wrong, for example), they'll issue corrected tax documents with the right information. These tax documents will have a "c" in their name (W-2c, for example) or be marked as "CORRECTED" to signify that they're a correction of previously issued documents. If received, you should consult with a tax professional on whether the correction is large enough to justify filing an amended tax return.

Ingredient List

Required:

- Original, incorrect tax return
- Form 1040-X
- Supporting documentation for your changes
- Tax filing software

Optional:

- The assistance of a tax professional (highly recommended)

Recipe

1. Determine whether you need to file an amended tax return. In general, it's good practice (and could help you avoid penalties) to file an amended tax return if any of the following will materially impact either the tax liability or tax refund originally reported on your tax return:
   a. Errors
   b. Omissions
   c. "Corrected" or newly-issued tax documents that weren't included in your original tax return filing
2. Determine whether it's too late to file an amended tax return. You generally have three years from the original due date of your tax return (including extensions) to file an amended return if it results in you receiving a refund. However, the IRS isn't one to turn down free money, so there's no time limit if you're amending a tax return to report additional income (which may cause you to generate a tax liability that you may owe interest and penalties on).
3. Gather supporting documentation. You'll need to attach the documents supporting your amendment to form 1040-X: the IRS wants to know exactly why you're filing this amendment. If you made an error or omission, you can attach the original document you received relating to these misentered/missed amounts. If you receive corrected tax documents, attach those to justify your adjustments.
4. Complete and file form 1040-X (ideally with the help of a tax professional). There are three main columns on Form 1040-X: column A reports the original amounts entered on your tax return, column C reports the corrected amounts, and column B reports the difference between the two. Follow the instructions on the form carefully (or let a tax professional do it for you) and provide a thorough explanation of your changes in "part III" of form 1040-X. Remember to attach your supporting documentation.

5. Keep a copy of both the form 1040-X and supporting documentation, and save the confirmation of either mailing or electronic filing of your amended tax return.

6. A similar process is followed if you must amend your state tax returns as well; check the specific guidelines for your state for more information.

Recap

1. Identify whether you need to file an amended tax return.
2. Determine whether you're still within the time window for filing an amended tax return.
3. Gather supporting documentation for your amendments.
4. Complete form 1040-X (ideally with the help of a tax professional), ensure to provide a thorough explanation for the changes made, and attach your supporting documentation.
5. Either mail your amended tax return to the IRS or file it electronically. Whichever method you choose, save a confirmation that it was either mailed or filed.
6. If you live in a state with income taxes, you'll likely need to file an amended state tax return as well. Follow your state's specific guidelines for this.

Chapter 10
Retirement

10.1 How to Begin Drawing Your Social Security Benefits

Setup Time	Maintenance Time	Function
1–2 Hours	N/A	Manage Money

You're closing in on retirement! The only problem? You don't know how to access your Social Security benefits, which you've earned after paying a lifetime of taxes. This recipe will walk you through how to begin drawing your social security benefits and discuss whether you should take them as soon as possible or wait.

Essential Terminology

Social Security Benefits: Payments provided by the Social Security Administration (SSA) to eligible individuals, including retirees, disabled individuals, and surviving spouses or dependents. The benefits are based on your earnings history and the age you elect to start receiving your benefits.
Full Retirement Age (FRA): The age you become eligible to receive your "full" Social Security benefit. Your FRA is 67 if you were born in 1960 or later, otherwise, it's 66 if you were born

earlier. Note that, especially if Social Security funds are stretched, this age is subject to change in the future. See the full benefits chart here: https://www.ssa.gov/benefits/retirement/planner/agereduction.html

Early Retirement: Choosing to receive your Social Security benefits before reaching your FRA, which results in reduced monthly payments. The earliest you can start your benefits is at age 62.

Delayed Retirement: Postponing your Social Security benefits until after your FRA, which can increase your monthly benefit amount. Your benefit amount stops increasing after age 70.

Ingredient List

Required:

- Social Security number (both you and your spouse, if any)
- Work history
- Bank account information for direct deposit

Recipe

1. Determine your full retirement age (FRA) based on your birth year. If you were born in 1960 or later, it's age 67. If you were born earlier, use this chart from the Social Security Administration to calculate your FRA: https://www.ssa.gov/benefits/retirement/planner/agereduction.html

2. Weigh your options. You can claim benefits as early as age 62, but your benefit increases every year you delay it until age 70. It's a deeply personal decision you need to talk over with your family, but I skew towards taking your benefit earlier than later. Why? A dollar at 62 is worth more than a dollar at 70. The older you get, the more difficult it becomes to use money on memorable experiences like travel. You can apply for social security benefits up to four months before your desired benefits start date, so the remainder of the recipe should be followed within that window of time.

3. Once you've made your decision, gather all the documents and information you'll need to make an account with ssa.gov. This includes:
   a. Your and your spouse's Social Security numbers.
   b. Your and your spouse's date and place of birth.
   c. Place of marriage (city, state, and country if outside the USA).
   d. US military service duty, branch, and dates (if any).
   e. Employer details for the current year and prior two years (employer name and employment start and end dates).
   f. Self-employment details for the current year and prior two years (business type and total net income).
   g. Bank account information for direct deposit.
4. Create an online account at ssa.gov. This will grant you access to your Social Security statements, estimate your benefits, and apply for benefits.
5. If you're still on the fence about when you should take your benefits, use the benefits estimator tool in your ssa.gov account to see what you'd receive based on when you decide to claim your benefits.
6. Apply for your benefits either online through your ssa.gov profile or by visiting your local social security office.
7. Await confirmation. After submitting your application, it'll be reviewed by the SSA. Once approved, you'll receive a confirmation letter detailing the amount and start date of your benefits.

Recap

1. Determine your full retirement age (FRA) based on your birth year.
2. Weigh your options, including early or delayed retirement.
3. Four months before you plan to start your benefits, gather the information and documents you need to open an ssa.gov online account.
4. Create an online account with ssa.gov.
5. Estimate your benefits using their online tools.
6. Apply for benefits, and await a confirmation letter.

10.2   How and When You're Required to Draw from Your Retirement Accounts

Setup Time	Maintenance Time	Function
45 Minutes	N/A	Manage Money

If you read Section 9.1, you know the only two certainties in life are death and taxes. Well, the government wants to make sure the latter applies to *all* your financial accounts, even your tax-advantaged retirement accounts. To ensure this happens, they have special distribution requirements for accounts like IRAs and 401(k)s. This recipe will tell you exactly what those are and how to stay compliant with them.

Essential Terminology

Tax-Advantaged Accounts: Special investment accounts, generally geared toward retirement savings, that provide certain tax benefits, like tax-deferred or tax-free growth. Examples include IRAs and 401(k)s.

Traditional IRA: A self-managed retirement account (IRA stands for "Individual Retirement Account") that allows you to deduct contributions from your taxable income in the year they're made, but you owe taxes on these funds when they're withdrawn in retirement. In other words, it saves you taxes *today* in return for a tax on your earnings *tomorrow*.

401(k): A retirement plan offered by non-government, non-healthcare employers that allows employees to invest a portion of their salary on a pre-tax basis. This means, much like a traditional IRA detailed in Section 2.2, the money contributed to your 401(k) is deducted from your taxable income the year it's contributed, but it's taxed at the same tax rate as your ordinary income when you withdraw it in retirement. The funds within a 401(k) also grow tax free.

IRS: The Internal Revenue Service. This is the governmental agency in charge of taxation.

Required Minimum Distributions (RMDs): Once you reach a certain age (72 as of 2023), the IRS requires that you withdraw a minimum amount from "pre-tax" retirement accounts (like traditional IRAs and 401(k)s) each year. Why would they do this? Because you haven't paid taxes on this money yet distributions from these accounts are taxed.

RMD Penalty: The IRS penalty for failing to take your RMD is 50% of the amount not taken on time.

QCD: A qualified charitable distribution (QCD) is when you directly transfer funds from your IRA to a qualified charity. Starting at age 73, this amount counts toward your RMD for the year (up to certain limits). QCDs are not counted toward your income, and they also aren't classified as standard charitable contributions on your tax return: It's essentially like you never owned this money in the first place.

Ingredient List

Required:

- Be lucky enough to make it to your 70s
- Pre-tax retirement accounts

Optional:

- A retirement planning professional to ensure you're doing this correctly

Recipe

1. Concept of RMDs: As we discussed on previous pages, RMDs exist to ensure the IRS eventually collects taxes on the money inside your pre-tax investing accounts. Your RMD is calculated by dividing your retirement account balance by a life expectancy factor provided by the IRS.

2. Don't miss your RMDs: The penalty for not taking your RMDs is steep: If you fail to take all or part of your RMD, the IRS will fine you 50% of the amount not taken.

3. Which accounts are subject to RMDs: RMD rules apply to all employer-sponsored retirement plans and IRAs, excluding Roth IRAs (since you already paid taxes on your contributions, though inherited Roth IRAs are subject to RMDs). This means all the following accounts are subject to RMD rules:

   a. 401(k) plans (including Roth 401(k)s)
   b. 403(b) plans
   c. Profit-sharing plans
   d. 457(b) plans
   e. Thrift Savings Plan
   f. Traditional IRAs
   g. SEP IRAs
   h. SARSEPs
   i. SIMPLE IRAs
   j. Inherited Roth IRAs (meaning you received the account because you are the beneficiary of the deceased account owner)

4. When to take your RMD: The deadline to take your first RMD is April 1st of the year following the year in which you turn 72 years old. For following years, RMDs must be taken by December 31st. However, if you're still working after turning 73, you may be able to delay taking RMDs from certain workplace retirement plans.

   a. It's important to note that if you choose to wait until the April 1st deadline following the year in which you turn 72 to make your first RMD, you'll be required to make two RMDs that year (one by April 1st, the other by December 31st). This will likely push you into a higher tax bracket than you would be in if you split the RMDs up between both years.

5. How to take your RMD: There's the hard way to take your RMD, then there's the easy way. We'll go over both of them below:

   a. Hand calculation (the hard way): Manually calculate the RMDs required on all your retirement accounts by dividing the account balances as of December 31st of the previous year by the distribution value listed on the IRS RMD tables you can find here: https://www.irs.gov/retirement-plans/plan-participant-employee/required-minimum-distribution-worksheets.

   b. Automated withdrawals (the easy way): Most retirement plan administrators allow you to elect for automatic withdrawals of your RMD each year, which they calculate using the IRS RMD tables. Electing for automated withdrawals greatly reduces the risk that you'll accidentally forget to take your RMD.

6. What to do with the money: Once you receive your RMD, you're free to do basically whatever you want with the money. You could use it to pay for living expenses, gift it to family members, or allocate it toward other investments. However, please keep in mind that this money is taxed as ordinary income, so ensure you have enough money set aside to cover taxes (if they weren't automatically withheld when taking your RMD).

   a. Alternatively, if you have no use for your RMD and would rather gift it to charity, consider making a QCD (described in the essential terminology section).

Recap

1. Understand that RMDs will require you to distribute a percentage of nearly all retirement account funds (except Roth IRAs) every year starting at age 72.

2. Your first RMD is due April 1st of the year following the year in which you turn 72 years old. For following years, RMDs must be taken by December 31st.

3. Use automated withdrawals for your RMDs when possible, and to make tax time easier, elect to withhold taxes from your RMD (if allowed by your broker).

4. Use your RMD money as you see fit, or donate it to charity with a QCD.

10.3   How to Determine How Much You Should Spend Each Year in Retirement

Setup Time	Maintenance Time	Function
45 Minutes	N/A	Manage Money

The worst fear of many retirees is running out of money before they kick the bucket. Determining how much of your nest egg you can comfortably spend in each year of retirement is one of the most important aspects of late-life financial planning. This recipe will guide you through the process of determining an appropriate withdrawal rate for your retirement funds that balances your financial needs with your financial balances.

Essential Terminology

Withdrawal Rate: The percentage of your retirement savings you withdraw each year to cover your living expenses.

Traditional IRA: A self-managed retirement account (IRA stands for "Individual Retirement Account") that allows you to deduct contributions from your taxable income in the year they're made, but you owe taxes on these funds when they're withdrawn in retirement. In other words, it saves you taxes *today* in return for a tax on your earnings *tomorrow*.

401(k): A retirement plan offered by non-government, non-healthcare employers that allows employees to invest a portion of their salary on a pre-tax basis. This means, much like a traditional IRA detailed in Section 2.2, the money contributed to your 401(k) is deducted from your taxable income the year it's contributed, but it's taxed at the same tax rate as your ordinary income when you withdraw it in retirement. The funds within a 401(k) also grow tax-free.

Social Security Benefits: Payments provided by the Social Security Administration (SSA) to eligible individuals, including retirees, disabled individuals, and surviving spouses or dependents. The benefits are based on your earnings history and the age you elect to start receiving your benefits.

Required Minimum Distributions (RMDs): Once you reach a certain age (72 as of 2023), the IRS requires that you withdraw a minimum amount from "pre-tax" retirement accounts (like traditional IRAs and 401(k)s) each year. Why would they do this? Because you haven't paid taxes on this money yet and distributions from these accounts are taxed.

The 4% Rule: A retirement planning rule of thumb that states that as long as you withdraw 4% or less of your total retirement fund balance per year to live off of, and your retirement funds are invested 75% in stocks and 25% in bonds, there's a 98% chance (https://www.forbes.com/sites/wadepfau/2018/01/16/the-trinity-study-and-portfolio-success-rates-updated-to-2018/?sh=23ac23246860) that you can live off your investments comfortably for at least thirty years.

Ingredient List

Required:

- Retirement savings (and a knowledge of your account balances)
- Budget and expense analysis
- Knowledge of investment returns and inflation

Recipe

1. Evaluate your financial accounts. Add up the value of everything, from your bank accounts to brokerage accounts to IRAs to 401(k)s in order to get a clear picture of the total amount of money you have saved for retirement. Also make sure to note accounts that will have RMDs (see Section 10.2), as this will impact the order you decide to withdraw from your accounts. Also, add in any income you expect to receive during retirement. This could be from rental real estate, business ventures, or social security (see Section 10.1).

2. This is a bit morbid, but you must estimate your retirement duration. Based on factors like your (and your spouse's) age, life expectancy, and health, determine how long you'll need to rely on these funds. Skew more conservatively to ensure you don't run out of money by living longer than you originally estimated.

3. Analyze your expenses. If you keep a budget (see Section 1.4), you should already have a solid grasp on how much money you spend per year. Adjust it based on categories, like travel and healthcare, that are likely to increase in cost during retirement. Again, it's better to skew conservatively here and assume you'll spend more than less.

4. Do you want to leave a sizable inheritance? If so, you may want to avoid touching the accounts that will be most advantageous for your heirs to receive, like your Roth IRA.

5. Understand the impact of investment returns and inflation on your retirement portfolio. Based on your investment mix, how much do you expect your portfolio to grow each year? Also, how much value do you expect to lose each year due to inflation?

6. Determine your ideal withdrawal rate. As mentioned in Section 1.6, the 4% rule is a guideline widely used in retirement planning (yes, real retirement planning, not just early retirement planning). According to the 4% rule, as long as you withdraw 4% or less of your total retirement fund balance per year to live off of, and your retirement funds are invested 75% in stocks and 25% in bonds, there's a 98% chance (https://www .forbes.com/sites/wadepfau/2018/01/16/the-trinity-study-and-portfolio-success-rates-updated-to-2018/?sh=23ac23246860) that you can live off of your investments comfortably for at least 30 years. Again, this number should be adjusted based on your individual situation, and remember, you can't take your money with you to the grave.

7. Withdraw money from your least-tax-advantaged accounts first. Money inside of accounts like your traditional IRA and 401(k) grow tax free, while any taxable activity inside of a brokerage account is taxed. Let tax-free compounding work its magic by withdrawing from your least-tax-advantaged accounts first.

8. Monitor and adjust. As you test out your withdrawal rate, does it seem like too much? Too little? Adjust moving forward to maximize the utility of your money in your golden years.

Recap

1. Evaluate your retirement portfolio, and make note of any accounts that have RMDs.
2. Estimate the duration of your retirement.
3. Analyze your expenses, and project what they'll be in retirement.
4. Determine your ideal withdrawal rate. The 4% rule works well for retirement planning.
5. Withdraw money from your least-tax-advantaged accounts first.
6. Monitor and adjust your withdrawal rate if it seems like too much or too little.

10.4   How to Roll Over Old 401(k)s to an IRA

Setup Time	Maintenance Time	Function
1–2 Hours	N/A	Manage Money

Over the course of your career, you have worked for a number of different employers. Holding old 401(k) accounts with these employers isn't only an administrative burden, it can be downright costly financially. Consolidating your older 401(k)s into a single rollover IRA can simplify your retirement savings strategy while potentially saving you money on plan administration fees. This recipe will guide you through the process of rolling your old 401(k) accounts into a rollover IRA.

Essential Terminology

401(k): A retirement plan offered by non-government, non-healthcare employers that allows employees to invest a portion of their salary on a pre-tax basis. This means, much like a traditional IRA detailed in Section 2.2, the money contributed to your 401(k) is deducted from your taxable income the year it's contributed, but it's taxed at the same tax rate as your ordinary income when you withdraw it in retirement. The funds within a 401(k) also grow tax free.

Traditional IRA: A self-managed retirement account (IRA stands for "Individual Retirement Account") that allows you to deduct contributions from your taxable income in the year they're made, but you owe taxes on these funds when they're withdrawn in retirement. In other words, it saves you taxes *today* in return for a tax on your earnings *tomorrow*.

Rollover IRA: A self-managed retirement account that has the same tax advantages as a traditional IRA, but it's unique because it allows you to transfer money into it from old 401(k)s. This is an attractive option because it simplifies your account management and typically comes with lower fees and more investment choices than a 401(k).

Rollover: Moving funds from one retirement account to another without incurring taxes or penalties for early withdrawals. In this specific scenario of transferring funds from a 401(k) to an IRA, it'd be considered a "401(k) rollover."

Broker: It's a fancy way to refer to the company that hosts your brokerage account. Just like you associate "banks" like Chase, Wells Fargo, and Bank of America with checking accounts, you can associate "brokers" like Fidelity, Vanguard, and Charles Schwab with brokerage accounts. Brokers are specifically licensed to facilitate transactions on the stock market, whereas most "regular" banks aren't.

Ingredient List

Required:

- Computer (smartphone could work but it's not recommended)
- Account with a broker that offers rollover IRAs
- Old 401(k) account information

Recipe

1. Decide whether a 401(k) rollover is worth it for you. Often, but not always, rolling a 401(k) into an IRA will reduce your fees, grant you more investment choices, and simplify your account management.
2. Research and choose an IRA provider. The "Big 3" brokers of Fidelity, Vanguard, and Charles Schwab are all great options, especially if your other brokerage accounts and IRAs are already with one of them. Factors to consider when assessing rollover IRA providers are:
   a. Account fees (if any)
   b. Investment choices
   c. Customer service
   d. Platform ease of use
3. Open a rollover IRA with the broker you chose.
4. Initiate the 401(k) rollover by contacting your older 401(k) provider. Inform them that you wish to roll over your 401(k), and they'll walk you through the necessary steps.
   a. If you don't know who to contact, look for a company name on the most recent 401(k) statement you received. If you still can't find it, contact your old employer.
   b. If your 401(k) and rollover IRA are held by the same broker (Fidelity, for example), you can often initiate the rollover directly on the platform.
5. Choose your rollover method. There are two methods for rolling over funds from a 401(k) into an IRA: a direct rollover and an indirect rollover. Direct rollovers involve transferring funds directly from your 401(k) to your rollover IRA. Indirect rollovers require you to receive a distribution from your 401(k) in the form of a check, then you must deposit that check into your rollover IRA within a specified time frame (usually 60 days) to avoid penalties. Clearly, it's recommended to do a direct rollover whenever possible, as there's much less of a chance of anything going wrong.
6. Complete any final steps of the rollover process, then invest your money. After your funds are rolled over, there's a good chance

that some (or all) of your account will be cash. Since this is money you should ideally plan to hold for a while, it's important to ensure that it's fully invested.

7. Repeat this process for any other old 401(k)s to consolidate your accounts in one place.

Recap

1. Analyze factors such as account fees and investment choices for both your old 401(k) provider and potential rollover IRA broker to see if a rollover is worth it.
2. Choose a rollover IRA broker.
3. Contact your old 401(k) provider to initiate the rollover process; you'll likely have to fill out a couple of forms.
4. Elect to do a direct rollover, if possible, to avoid potential penalties and fees.
5. Once the rollover is completed, ensure the funds in your rollover IRA are fully invested.
6. Repeat this process for any other old 401(k)s to consolidate your accounts in one place.

Chapter 11
Charitable Giving

11.1   How to Report Charitable Donations on Your Tax Return

Setup Time	Maintenance Time	Function
30–60 Minutes	1 Hour per Year	Charitable Giving

Donating to your favorite charitable causes isn't only good for your soul, it can also be great for your wallet because of the potential tax benefits. Well, you're still donating more money than you'll be saving, but it's a nice extra incentive to help out causes you care about. In order to receive the tax benefits of giving to charity, you'll need to report them properly on your tax return: which is exactly what this recipe will guide you through.

Essential Terminology

IRS: The Internal Revenue Service. This is the governmental agency in charge of taxation.
Tax Return: The aggregation of the tax forms you fill out, which tells the government how much you made in a year, how much tax you already paid through withholdings, and how much you owe or are due as a refund.

Charitable Donations: Cash or material contributions made to qualified nonprofit organizations or charities. In order to qualify for a tax deduction, these donations must be made in the form of cash, property, or goods (you can't write off the value of your time while volunteering as a charitable contribution).

Tax Deduction: An expense (or donation, in this case) that reduces your total taxable income, resulting in lower taxes owed.

Standard Deduction: A set amount of money ($13,850 for single tax filers, $27,700 for married tax filers in 2023) that you can subtract from your income to lower your taxes, assuming you don't itemize your deductions.

Itemized Deductions: Specific expenses, like charitable donations, mortgage interest, and medical expenses that can help lower the amount of taxes you owe. It only makes sense to claim itemized deductions if, when totalled up, they exceed the amount of the standard deduction.

Ingredient List

Required:

- Qualified charities to donate to
- Donation receipts
- Enough itemized deductions to exceed the standard deduction

Recipe

1. If you want to make donations for tax purposes, see if it's even possible to claim a tax benefit for your situation. In order to receive a tax deduction for your charitable contributions, you need to itemize your deductions. In order to itemize your deductions, they have to (or should, at least) exceed the amount of your standard deduction (see amounts under the essential terminology section). If they don't, you'd be opting for a lower tax deduction by itemizing your deductions.

   a. To realistically exceed the standard contribution amount, you'll likely need to be able to donate money in the five-figures range to charity in a single year.

2. Determine the eligibility of the charitable organizations before you donate to them. In order for the donation to qualify as a tax-deductible expense, the charity must be listed in the IRS's tax-exempt organization database, which you can search here: https://www.irs.gov/charities-non-profits/tax-exempt-organization-search

3. Make your donations to qualified charities, and ensure you receive official receipts from them detailing the donation date and amount.

   a. If you receive anything of benefit in return for your donation (a dinner, experience, gift, etc.), the fair market value of that benefit should be deducted from your donation amount.

4. When filing your tax return, enter your charitable contributions on Schedule A. This is a tax form that lists your itemized deductions.

5. For large non-cash charitable donations (like if you donated your car or a large amount of stock—more on the stock donation piece in Section 11.2), you may need to complete Form 8283.

   a. This is a worksheet the IRS will pay close attention to, so it would be wise to enlist the help of a tax professional to complete this properly.

6. Give yourself a pat on the back: you just helped out a charity and secured yourself a tax deduction while you were at it!

Recap

1. Total up your non-charitable itemized deductions amounts, then subtract that number from the standard deduction to see if it's even realistic to receive a tax deduction for your charitable contributions. Your itemized deductions must be greater than your standard deduction for this to make sense.

2. Confirm the charitable organizations you want to give to are qualified charities by finding them in the IRS's database: https://www.irs.gov/charities-non-profits/tax-exempt-organization-search

3. Request receipts from the charities you donate to that detail the date and amount of the donation.

4. When filing your tax return, enter your charitable donations on Schedule A. Large non-cash donations may prompt you to complete form 8283.

11.2   How to Open a Donor-Advised Fund for Tax-Advantaged Giving

Setup Time	Maintenance Time	Function
30–60 Minutes	1 Hour per Year	Charitable Giving

If you read Section 11.1, you know that charitable donations can be a valuable method to save money on taxes while also helping out causes you support. However, as you also saw, it can be difficult to receive *any* tax benefit for charitable donations unless you donate a lot of money at once and exceed the standard deduction: we're talking donations of five figures plus in a single calendar year. For this reason, and also to avoid capital gains taxes (more on this shortly), many higher-net-worth individuals opt to frontload their charitable donations of five, six, or even seven figures by donating stock to their donor-advised fund (DAF). This recipe will show you how to open and effectively use a donor-advised fund to maximize the tax benefit of your charitable donations.

Essential Terminology

Donor Advised Fund (DAF): A special form of investing account held at a broker that is used to manage your charitable giving. Donors (you) contribute to their DAF, receive an immediate charitable tax deduction for the full amount they contributed in the year they made the contribution, choose whether to invest these funds within the account or leave them as cash, and determine when to make donations to qualified charities using these funds (does not have to be the same year as the contribution).

The DAF itself is a charitable entity, which is why you're allowed to claim the charitable tax deduction in full when you make your contribution, though you don't get additional tax deductions for the money that is given by the DAF to charities. You can contribute cash and stocks (which is a major benefit explained further in the recipe) to your DAF.

Qualified Charitable Organization: Nonprofit organizations recognized by the IRS as eligible to receive tax-deductible donations. Search the IRS database here: https://www.irs.gov/charities-non-profits/tax-exempt-organization-search.

IRS: The Internal Revenue Service. This is the governmental agency in charge of taxation.

Tax Return: The aggregation of the tax forms you fill out, which tells the government how much you made in a year, how much tax you already paid through withholdings, and how much you owe or are due as a refund.

Charitable Donations: Cash or material contributions made to qualified nonprofit organizations or charities. In order to qualify for a tax deduction, these donations must be made in the form of cash, property, or goods (you can't write off the value of your time while volunteering as a charitable contribution).

Tax Deduction: An expense (or donation, in this case) that reduces your total taxable income, resulting in lower taxes owed.

Standard Deduction: A set amount of money ($13,850 for single tax filers, $27,700 for married tax filers in 2023) that you can subtract from your income to lower your taxes, assuming you don't itemize your deductions.

Itemized Deductions: Specific expenses, like charitable donations, mortgage interest, and medical expenses that can help lower the amount of taxes you owe. It only makes sense to claim itemized deductions if, when totaled up, they exceed the amount of the standard deduction.

Capital Gains: The profit you make from selling an investment, such as stocks or index funds. For example: if you bought a stock for $100, and later sold it for $150, your capital gain would be $50. This $50 capital gain is the only part of this transaction that's taxed (your $100 "cost basis" isn't taxed). Capital gains on assets held for one year or less ("short-term capital gains") are taxed at your ordinary income tax rates (up to 37%), while long-term capital gains (assets that were sold after more than one year of you holding them) are taxed at a much lower rate (15% for most people, 20% is the highest rate). Note that these rates are subject to change, but are current as of 2023.

Broker: It's a fancy way to refer to the company that hosts your brokerage account. Just like you associate "banks" like Chase, Wells Fargo, and Bank of America with checking accounts, you can associate "brokers" like Fidelity, Vanguard, and Charles Schwab with brokerage accounts. Brokers are specifically licensed to facilitate transactions on the stock market, whereas most "regular" banks aren't.

Ingredient List

Required:

- Computer or smartphone
- The desire to donate to charity

Optional:

- Brokerage account with a "Big 3" broker (Fidelity, Vanguard, and Charles Schwab—see Section 2.1), as they all offer DAFs
- Highly appreciated stock
- The ability to donate a large lump sum (five to seven figures) in one year to maximize your tax benefit

Recipe

1. Understand how DAFs work. Here's a high-level overview of the process of using a DAF:
   a. In a year where you have higher-than-typical taxable income, you may opt to make a single large charitable donation. We'll use $100,000 as an example.

b. Instead of sending this directly to a charity as cash, you opt to use a DAF because:

   i. You want the charitable tax deduction this year, but you want to spread your donations out over the coming years.

   ii. You want to donate highly-appreciated stocks that you hold in your brokerage account instead of cash. Why? If you *sold* your stocks, you'd be taxed on your capital gains. However, if you *donate* them, you can claim their full value as a tax deduction, and you avoid paying capital gains taxes. It's a double-win from a tax perspective.

c. You contribute your $100,000 of stocks to your DAF and claim your charitable tax deduction of $100,000 (which far exceeds the standard deduction).

   i. Since your DAF is considered a charitable entity, you're not allowed to withdraw these funds for personal use.

d. You decide you want to give $10,000 of this DAF money per year to your favorite charity. To ensure these funds grow slightly over the years while waiting to be donated, you choose the conservative investment strategy offered by your DAF.

e. You donate this money when you see fit (but don't get any additional charitable tax deductions).

2. Decide whether a DAF is right for you. Anybody can open a DAF, but, as you can see in Step 1, they're generally used by those who want to do one or both of the following:

   a. Donate appreciated stock (instead of cash, though that's also an option) to charity.

   b. Make a five-figure-plus contribution to your DAF in a single year to maximize the tax benefit, then have the ability to stretch your donations (using the funds from your initial contribution) out over a longer time horizon.

3. Choose a DAF provider. Generally, it's easiest to open one where you have your brokerage account, because this allows you to easily make contributions to your DAF from your brokerage account. Each of the "Big 3" brokers (Fidelity, Vanguard, or

Charles Schwab) offers DAFs. Before opening a DAF, consider factors like fees, investment options, minimum contribution requirements, and the quality of customer service.

4. Choose an investment strategy. When completing your application, you'll likely be asked how to invest the funds inside of your DAF. As detailed in the essential terminology section of this recipe, though you claim the full amount of your contribution as a charitable tax deduction the year you make it, you can wait to distribute your funds to charities. While these funds are sitting in the account, they can be invested (in both conservative and aggressive strategies) and grow before you eventually donate them to the charities of your choice (however, it must be noted that you will not be given any additional charitable deduction if these funds grow).

5. Contribute to your DAF. As you saw in the example in step 1, your contributions should ideally:
    a. Be made in a large lump sum above the amount of the standard deduction during a year that you expect to have (or have had, if you're contributing to your DAF late in the year), a larger-than-typical amount of taxable income.
    b. Consist of highly-appreciated stocks, not cash. This will allow you to avoid capital gains taxes on these stocks while claiming their full value as a charitable tax deduction. If your DAF is connected to your brokerage account, you'll have the option to donate stocks on your contribution page. To ensure you select the right stocks to donate, I'd recommend either contacting the customer support team of your DAF or a financial advisor who is experienced in using DAFs.

6. Determine when and where you want to donate these funds. Though there's no specific requirement on how quickly you need to donate the funds inside of your DAF, you want to ensure this money actually gets into the hands of the charities you want to support, so it's good practice to put together a distribution plan. If you contributed $100,000 to your DAF, maybe you'll gift $10,000 per year for 10 years, maybe it's $20,000 over 5 years,

or maybe it's $50,000 over 2 years. The choice is yours, and again, you receive no additional benefit when you make these donations (even if the value of your funds increases because of your investment choices), so the tax-planning aspect of DAFs ends after you make the contribution to your account.

7. Make your charitable donations via your DAF. Most DAFs will have online portals that allow you to transfer funds directly from your DAF to a qualified charity; otherwise, you may need to fill out a form to initiate the donation.

8. Monitor your DAF, and make additional contributions. Over time, ensure you're comfortable with your DAF's fees, the performance of your investing strategy, and the pace of your charitable donations. If another window pops up where it makes sense to make another contribution to your DAF, follow this same recipe again from steps 5 to 8.

Recap

1. Understand how DAFs work, and whether opening one would make sense for you.

2. Choose a DAF provider, ideally one offered by your current broker, and complete the online application.

3. Make your initial contribution to your DAF, and note this amount as it will be counted as a charitable tax deduction on your tax return for that year. Ideally, contribute highly-appreciated stock in a year where you'll have a higher-than-typical income.

4. Plan a donation strategy for the funds inside your DAF.

5. Use your DAF's online portal to make donations to qualified charities using the funds inside your DAF. Note, you will not receive any additional tax benefits when making these donations.

6. Monitor your DAF, and make additional contributions when you see fit.

Chapter 12

Insurance

12.1 How to Use an HSA as an Extra Retirement Account

Setup Time	Maintenance Time	Function
30 Minutes	15 Minutes per Year	Save and Make Money

Preparing for retirement by contributing to "normal" retirement accounts like IRAs and workplace retirement plans is fine and dandy, but there is a "secret" retirement account you may have access to that can really supercharge your retirement savings. It's called a health savings account (HSA for short), and even though the name sounds kind of bland, it offers a unique suite of tax advantages you can use to save money today while supercharging your retirement savings. This recipe will teach you who's eligible to open an HSA, and, if you are, how to use it to your advantage.

Essential Terminology

Health Savings Account (HSA): A tax-advantaged investing (yes, you can invest in it despite its name) account available to those covered by a high-deductible health plan. Like a traditional

IRA, the money you contribute to your HSA is tax deductible, the funds inside the account grow tax free, and the unique part of HSAs is that money withdrawn from the account to pay for qualified medical expenses is also tax free. When you reach age 65, the ability to withdraw your funds tax free to pay for medical expenses remains, but you also unlock the ability to withdraw your funds for any purposes without penalty (though you are taxed on them). So, your HSA can essentially be seen as a beefed-up traditional IRA with a slightly later withdrawal date. However, HSAs have lower annual contribution limits than IRAs. Your plan administrator will provide you with up-to-date contribution limits depending on whether you have single or family coverage. Depending on your HSA plan administrator, funds inside your HSA can typically be invested into the same assets your other investing accounts have access to.

High-Deductible Health Plan (HDHP): A type of health insurance with higher deductibles and lower premiums than traditional health insurance. To be eligible to contribute to an HSA, you must be enrolled in an HDHP. The reasoning behind this rule is that you'd use your HSA funds to pay for your medical expenses up to this higher deductible if needed.

Tax Deduction: An expense (or donation, in this case) that reduces your total taxable income, resulting in lower taxes owed.

Traditional IRA: A self-managed retirement account (IRA stands for "Individual Retirement Account") that allows you to deduct contributions from your taxable income in the year they're made, but you owe taxes on these funds when they're withdrawn in retirement. In other words, it saves you taxes *today* in return for a tax on your earnings *tomorrow*.

Broker: It's a fancy way to refer to the company that hosts your brokerage account. Just like you associate "banks" like Chase, Wells Fargo, and Bank of America with checking accounts, you can associate "brokers" like Fidelity, Vanguard, and Charles

Schwab with brokerage accounts. Brokers are specifically licensed to facilitate transactions on the stock market, whereas most "regular" banks aren't.

Ingredient List

Required:

- You're enrolled in an HDHP that makes you eligible to open an HSA
- Employer-sponsored HSA or HSA broker
- Enough extra cash to contribute to an HSA

Optional:

- An understanding of the different investment choices (see Section 2.5)

Recipe

1. Confirm that you're eligible for an HSA. Check with your employer or insurance provider to ensure that you're enrolled in an HDHP that allows you to participate in an HSA.
2. Open an HSA. If your healthcare plan is through your employer, they may require that you open an HSA through their recommended provider. If this isn't an option, you can open an HSA on your own with one of the "Big 3" brokers (Fidelity, Vanguard, or Charles Schwab).
   a. In my experience, HSAs opened through the brokers tend to be much more flexible with investment choices than those through employer-recommended providers (though sometimes these are operated through one of the "Big 3" brokers).
3. Contribute to your HSA. If your healthcare plan is through your employer, these contributions will likely be taken directly from your paychecks. If not, log into your HSA and make a

contribution directly from your bank or brokerage account (a very similar process to contributing to a brokerage account, see Section 2.1). Note that contribution limits are subject to change each year, and they're typically lower than what you're allowed to contribute to an IRA. Your HSA provider will inform you of the current year's limits (typically shown on your account page and while making contributions). As of 2023, the HSA contribution limit for those with self-only health insurance coverage is $3,850, and it's $7,750 for those with family health insurance coverage.

4. Decide whether to save or invest your HSA funds. If you want to use the HSA for its intended purpose, as a tax-advantaged savings account to pay for medical expenses, it would make sense to keep your funds in cash or low-risk investments. If you plan to use your HSA as an extra retirement account, it may make sense to invest these funds more aggressively.

5. Track and manage your HSA. Do your contributions and investments align with your financial goals? If not, adjust accordingly.

6. When you're closing in on retirement, plan your withdrawal strategy. Do you want to keep these funds to pay for healthcare costs tax free? Or will you withdraw them for everyday spending and get taxed on them once you reach age 65?

Recap

1. Determine your eligibility for an HSA (you must be enrolled in an HDHP).

2. Open an HSA through either your health insurance's recommended provider or a broker.

3. Contribute to your HSA (keep contribution limits in mind).

4. Decide whether you want to use your HSA for healthcare costs or retirement savings, and save/invest the funds inside your HSA accordingly.

5. Track and manage your HSA.

6. When you're closing in on retirement, decide whether you want to use these funds for medical expenses or withdraw them for everyday expenses (and pay income taxes) once you turn age 65.

12.2   How to Obtain Health Insurance When It Isn't Provided by Your Employer (When Turning 26)

Setup Time	Maintenance Time	Function
30 Minutes–2 Hours	30 Minutes per Year	Protect Your Money

Turning 26 is the *opposite* of a good time: for one, you realize you're officially getting old because you're closer to 30 than you are to 20, and secondly, you get kicked off of your parents' health insurance coverage. The latter isn't that big of a deal if your employer offers a healthcare plan you can participate in, but what if they don't? As someone who turned 26 without access to an employer-sponsored healthcare plan, I personally know how much of a pain this process can be, especially if you have no guidance. Though each state has its own healthcare marketplaces and the instructions won't be exactly the same for everyone, the goal of this recipe is to give you some of that guidance.

Essential Terminology

Health Insurance: A form of insurance that helps you cover medical expenses, including doctor visits, hospitalizations, medications, surgeries, and preventative care. However, exactly what care is covered, and how much money you have to pay out of pocket for the care, is highly dependent on what type of health insurance you have.

Deductible: The amount of money you have to pay out of pocket for a medical procedure/service before insurance helps pay for it. For example, a $4,000 deductible means you have to pay $4,000 of your own money before insurance steps in to help with the costs exceeding $4,000.

Open Enrollment Period: A designated period in the fall (the dates for 2023 are November 1st through December 15th) during which individuals can enroll in or make changes to their health insurance plans.

Special Enrollment Period: A time outside of the annual open enrollment period when you can sign up for health insurance. Special enrollment periods are available when you undergo a major life event, such as moving states, getting married, having a baby, adopting a child, if your household income falls below a certain amount, or if you lose health coverage (like you do when you turn 26) (https://www.healthcare.gov/glossary/special-enroll ment-period/). Depending on the type of event, you may either have 60 days before or 60 days after the event to enroll in a new health insurance plan.

Health Insurance Marketplace: A marketplace where you can compare and enroll in different health insurance plans. Each state has its own marketplace that you can find by visiting https://www .healthcare.gov/ and entering your state of residence in the drop-down menu on the "get coverage" tab.

Premiums: Monthly payments you make to your health insur-ance provider to maintain your health insurance coverage. This is a fixed cost that you are obligated to pay whether you use your health insurance or not.

Copayments: Also known as "copays," this is a fixed amount that you pay when receiving certain medical services or buying pre-scription drugs. This amount will be less than the services/drugs cost, and your health insurance will pay the rest of the bill. The amount of the copay depends on your health insurance plan.

Network Coverage: Refers to the group of healthcare providers, hospitals, clinics, and pharmacies that have agreed to provide ser-vices to individuals covered by a specific health insurance plan. This essentially pigeonholes you to working with this set group of healthcare providers, since using out-of-network providers may result in reduced insurance coverage and higher costs for you.

Health Savings Account (HSA): A tax-advantaged investing (yes, you can invest in it despite its name) account available to those covered by a high-deductible health plan. Like a traditional IRA, the money you contribute to your HSA is tax deductible, the funds inside the account grow tax free, and the unique part of HSAs is that money withdrawn from the account to pay for qualified medical expenses is also tax free. When you reach age 65, the ability to withdraw your funds tax free to pay for medical expenses remains, but you also unlock the ability to withdraw your funds for any purposes without penalty (though you are taxed on them). **High-Deductible Health Plan (HDHP)**: A type of health insurance with higher deductibles and lower premiums than traditional health insurance. To be eligible to contribute to an HSA, you must be enrolled in an HDHP. The reasoning behind this rule is that you'd use your HSA funds to pay for your medical expenses up to this higher deductible if needed.

Ingredient List

Required:

- Computer or smartphone
- Social Security number or ITIN
- Personal ID (driver's license or passport)
- Proof of address (utility bill, signed lease agreement, etc.)

Recipe

1. A few months before turning 26, determine whether you're eligible for a special enrollment period. Assuming you don't turn 26 during the open enrollment period, you'll need to utilize a special enrollment period to get health insurance coverage. Special enrollment periods are available when you experience qualifying life events, such as:
   a. Losing health insurance coverage (because you turned 26, for example, or you lost access to employer-sponsored healthcare)
   b. Getting married or divorced
   c. Having a child
   d. Moving to a new state

2. Create a healthcare.gov account. Go to https://www.healthcare .gov/screener/ to confirm that you are indeed eligible for a special enrollment period and, if so, create an account.

3. Compare healthcare plan options. After creating your health care.gov account, you should be brought to your state's health insurance marketplace. If not, go to https://www.healthcare .gov/get-coverage/ and select your state in the dropdown menu. You'll see a list of health plans to choose from. Compare health insurance (and dental, vision, etc.) plans based on factors like:
   a. Monthly premiums
   b. Deductibles
   c. Copayments
   d. Network coverage
   e. Prescription drug coverage
   f. Whether the plan is HSA-eligible (must be an HDHP)

4. If offered, consider enlisting the help of an insurance agent. When I moved to Colorado and started the health insurance signup process, I was put in touch with an insurance agent who specialized in helping people choose and sign up for insurance on Colorado's state health insurance marketplace. At least in Colorado, they're paid by the state, not you, so their services are completely free. Just send them what you're looking for in a health plan and they'll send you what they believe are the best options available. My agent collected my necessary documents and even completed the signup process for me. This made what was a very confusing process a lot easier, so I can't recommend using one enough (if available).
   a. Note: I was a resident of Minnesota on my 26th birthday and wasn't offered help by an insurance agent when signing up for a health plan there, so this seems to be a state-specific service. However, the insurance agent I used moving to Colorado is licensed in twelve states, so Colorado likely isn't the only one offering these services.

5. Finalize your healthcare choices and submit your application(s). Ensure your coverage date starts as soon as possible (or at least as soon as possible after your coverage under your parents' plan

ends) so you don't have a gap in coverage. Also, ensure you don't only enroll in health coverage, but dental and vision as well.

6. Congrats! If it were up to me, this would be the true marker for officially entering adulthood. You'll have the ability (or may be forced to) change your healthcare coverage during the annual open enrollment period. I added that "may be forced to" in there because your plan could be discontinued, forcing you to choose another health insurance plan during open enrollment. This happened to me and is no big deal, but still something you need to be aware of. If this is the case, your insurance provider will do everything in their power to make sure they notify you about this.

Recap

1. Determine whether you're eligible for a special enrollment period by entering your information into https://www.healthcare .gov/screener/. Ideally, do this two months before you turn 26.
2. Compare healthcare plan options on your state's health insurance marketplace.
3. If offered, consider utilizing an insurance agent.
4. Finalize your healthcare choices and submit your application(s). Also, ensure you don't only enroll in health coverage, but dental and vision as well.

12.3   How to Use an HSA as an Extra Retirement Account

Setup Time	Maintenance Time	Function
30 Minutes–1 Hour	30 Minutes per Year	Protect Your Money

It's almost scary how much health insurance is tied to your place of work in the USA: as of 2021, the census reported that 54.3% of the US population was covered by employer-based health insurance (https://www.census.gov/library/publications/2022/demo/p60-278.html). The upside of this is that, if you are one of those who are lucky enough to be offered health insurance through your job, it's a much simpler process than signing up for health insurance on your own (see Section 12.2). This recipe will walk you through how to sign up for health insurance when it's offered by your employer.

Essential Terminology

Health Insurance: A form of insurance that helps you cover medical expenses, including doctor visits, hospitalizations, medications, surgeries, and preventative care. However, exactly what care is covered, and how much money you have to pay out of pocket for the care, is highly dependent on what type of health insurance you have.

Employer-Sponsored Health Insurance: Health insurance plans offered to employees by their employer. The business typically pays for a large portion of the cost, and any premium payments made by employees come out of their paychecks tax free.

Premiums: Monthly payments you make to your health insurance provider to maintain your health insurance coverage. This is a fixed cost that you are obligated to pay whether you use your health insurance or not.

Copayments: Also known as "copays," this is a fixed amount that you pay when receiving certain medical services or buying prescription drugs. This amount will be less than the services/drugs cost, and your health insurance will pay the rest of the bill. The amount of the copay depends on your health insurance plan.

Network Coverage: Refers to the group of healthcare providers, hospitals, clinics, and pharmacies that have agreed to provide services to individuals covered by a specific health insurance plan. This essentially pigeonholes you to working with this set group of healthcare providers, since using out-of-network providers may result in reduced insurance coverage and higher costs for you.

Health Savings Account (HSA): A tax-advantaged investing (yes, you can invest in it despite its name) account available to those covered by a high-deductible health plan. Like a traditional IRA, the money you contribute to your HSA is tax deductible, the funds inside the account grow tax free, and the unique part of HSAs: money withdrawn from the account to pay for qualified medical expenses is also tax free. When you reach age 65, the ability to withdraw your funds tax free to pay for medical expenses remains, but you also unlock the ability to withdraw your funds for any purposes without penalty (though you are taxed on them).

High-Deductible Health Plan (HDHP): A type of health insurance with higher deductibles and lower premiums than traditional health insurance. To be eligible to contribute to an HSA, you must be enrolled in an HDHP. The reasoning behind this rule is that you'd use your HSA funds to pay for your medical expenses up to this higher deductible if needed. HDHPs can either be HMOs or PPOs (see following definitions).

Health Maintenance Organizations (HMOs): A type of health insurance plan where you choose a primary care doctor from a network of doctors and need to get referrals to see specialists. They often offer lower premiums and out-of-pocket costs when making in-network visits. HMOs generally don't cover out-of-network care unless it's an emergency.

Preferred Provider Organization (PPO): A type of health insurance plan that gives you more flexibility in choosing healthcare providers, allowing you to visit both in-network and out-of-network doctors, but they usually have higher premiums and deductibles. You don't need to select a primary care doctor, and you don't need a referral to see a specialist.

Deductible: The amount of money you have to pay out of pocket for a medical procedure/service before insurance helps pay for it. For example, a $4,000 deductible means you have to pay $4,000 of your own money before insurance steps in to help with the costs exceeding $4,000.

Open Enrollment Period: A designated period in the fall (the dates for 2023 are November 1st through December 15th) during which individuals can enroll in or make changes to their health insurance plans.

Special Enrollment Period: A time outside of the annual open enrollment period when you can sign up for health insurance. Special enrollment periods are available when you undergo a major life event, such as moving states, getting married, having a baby, adopting a child, if your household income falls below a certain amount, or if you lose health coverage (like you do when you turn 26) (https://www.healthcare.gov/glossary/special-enroll ment-period/). Depending on the type of event, you may either have 60 days before or 60 days after the event to enroll in a new health insurance plan.

Ingredient List

Required:

- You work for an employer that offers health insurance benefits (you typically need to be a full-time, not part-time, employee)
- Personal ID (driver's license, passport)
- Employee ID

Recipe

1. Confirm that your employer offers health insurance plans for its employees. If you're not told during the hiring process (which you should be), the quickest way to find out is by asking either your boss or the HR department.
2. Confirm your eligibility. Some employers limit health coverage to full-time employees and/or require a waiting period before coverage begins.
3. Enroll during the open enrollment period. Most employers have an annual open enrollment period in the fall in which employees are free to enroll in or make updates to their health insurance

plans for the upcoming calendar year. The exact sign-up process is different for every employer, but you'll typically log in through an employee benefits web portal that allows you to compare and enroll in health insurance plans. Your employer should offer plenty of resources to help you understand this sign-up process.

   a. If you need to enroll in health insurance before the open enrollment period, ask HR if you qualify for a special enrollment period. These are triggered when you undergo qualifying life events, like losing health coverage (for example: leaving another job where you had health insurance, or turning 26 and losing your parents' health coverage), getting married, getting divorced, or having a child.

4. Analyze various factors to confirm you're choosing the right health insurance coverage for your situation. Common factors include:
   a. Monthly premiums
   b. Deductibles
   c. Copayments
   d. Network coverage
   e. Prescription drug coverage
   f. Whether the plan is HSA-eligible (must be an HDHP)
5. Submit enrollment forms and any required documentation by the open enrollment period (or special enrollment period) deadline.
6. Familiarize yourself with your health plan, and utilize it. Obtain your insurance card, choose a primary doctor (if required), and schedule check-up appointments.

Recap

1. Confirm that your employer offers health insurance coverage for their employees and that you qualify for it.
2. Enroll during the open enrollment period, or if health insurance is needed before then, see if you qualify for a special enrollment period.
3. Compare and analyze the different factors of your prospective health insurance plans.

4. Submit your enrollment requests and, when approved, start using your health coverage.

5. Bonus: read Section 12.2 to see how much easier you have it than those who have to sign up for health coverage on their own in the marketplace.

12.4   How to Obtain Homeowner's Insurance

Setup Time	Maintenance Time	Function
1–2 Hours	1 Hour per Year	Protect Your Money

If you plan on using a mortgage to buy a home, you'll also need to plan on buying homeowner's insurance. It's a requirement set forth by mortgage lenders because they want to make sure you can still pay them if something catastrophic happens to the house. Even if this wasn't the case, or you own your home outright, it's still a great idea to insure what will probably be the largest purchase of your life. If you owned a $500,000 house, and a fire burned it down, I'm willing to bet you'd rather not try to muster up a couple hundred thousand dollars of your own money to rebuild it when an insurance company could've handled it instead. This recipe will go over the ins and outs of acquiring homeowner's insurance.

Essential Terminology

Homeowner's Insurance: A type of insurance that provides financial protection to homeowners against damage or loss to their property and belongings. Coverage is typically included for the physical structure of the home, your personal belongings, liability protection, and living expenses if you're unable to live in your home during covered events.

Dwelling Coverage: The portion of your homeowner's insurance that protects the physical structure of your home. This includes walls, roof, floors, and built-in appliances.

Personal Property Coverage: The portion of your homeowner's insurance that protects your personal belongings, which include items like furniture, electronics, clothing, and appliances, against damage or theft.

Liability Coverage: The portion of your homeowner's insurance that provides you with financial protection if someone is injured on your property or if you accidentally cause damage to someone else's property. It helps cover legal expenses if someone were to sue you for either of these things.

Mortgage: A loan to buy a house; the house itself serves as collateral for the loan. This means, if you fail to make your loan payments, the bank that issued your mortgage could potentially take ownership of your home.

Ingredient List

Required:

- A home to insure (duh)
- Property information (square footage, construction materials, and more)
- Details of valuable belongings (estimated value, receipts, photos/videos, etc.)
- Information on additional structures (garage, shed, barn, etc.)
- Information on home security features (alarms and smoke detectors)
- Claims history (if any)

Recipe

Note: This recipe assumes you are in, or about to start, the home-buying process.

1. When you begin your home search, also start researching insurance providers. Mortgage lenders require that you have a home insurance policy ready before you close on a house. It's wise to take this time to compare companies and coverage options

before you begin the closing process on a house and are forced to rush this.

2. Narrow down your top two or three insurance providers, and, when you find a home you're attempting to close on, request quotes from them using the exact details of the property.

3. Compare these quotes based on factors like coverage limits, deductibles, premiums, and any additional benefits of each plan. *Important*: If you live in an area prone to natural disasters like fires, floods, or earthquakes, these are not typically covered in a standard homeowner's insurance policy. You may need to contact another insurance provider to secure coverage for these events.
   a. Note: You may receive discounts if you bundle your home insurance with another type of insurance offered by the insurance company, such as auto insurance.

4. Review the policy terms and conditions before making your final decision. It's important that you're actually able to use your insurance when it's needed, so make sure you read through and fully understand your policy.

5. Select your winning policy and obtain a "proof of insurance" document from them. You'll need to present this document to your mortgage lender to get the mortgage approved and finalize your home purchase.

6. After officially completing the home purchase, finalize your homeowner's insurance policy. You'll make regular premium payments to maintain your coverage.

7. If qualifying damage ever occurs to your property or belongings, file a claim with your insurance company to get some (or all) of the damages reimbursed to you.

Recap

1. Start comparing insurance providers when you begin your home search.

2. When you've found a home you want to close on, ask for quotes from a couple of different insurance providers.

3. Compare the quotes to find the one that works best for your situation.

4. Select your winning policy and request a "proof of insurance" document from them. Present this document to your mortgage lender to officially be approved for your mortgage and close on your home.
5. After closing on your home, finalize your homeowner's insurance policy and start making premium payments.
6. Make claims if any qualifying damage occurs.

12.5   How to Obtain Renter's Insurance

Setup Time	Maintenance Time	Function
1–2 Hours	30 Minutes per Year	Protect Your Money

Renting a home or apartment doesn't come with quite as many risks as owning a property does, but there is still potential for a massively negative financial outcome if you lost all your belongings in something like an apartment fire, or somebody sues you for an injury that occurred on the property you're renting. Because of this, many apartment managers and landlords actually require that you obtain renter's insurance if you rent from them. Even if it's not a requirement where you live, it's still something you should consider. This recipe will walk you through the ins and outs of obtaining renter's insurance.

Essential Terminology

Renter's Insurance: A type of insurance that provides coverage for personal property and liability for damages that occur within a rented property. In addition to these main two areas of coverage, it can also provide additional living expenses if your rental unit is rendered unlivable due to a qualifying event.
Personal Property: Your personal belongings, such as furniture, electronics, clothing, kitchenware, and anything else of value in your rental unit.

Liability Coverage: Protection against claims or lawsuits filed against you for injury or property damage that occurred within your rented property.

Deductible: The amount you're responsible for paying with your own money before insurance coverage kicks in.

Premium: The cost you pay for your insurance coverage, usually on a monthly, bi-annual, or annual basis.

Ingredient List

Required:

- You're renting, or plan to rent, a house or apartment
- Basic information about your rented property
- Inventory of your personal belongings.

Recipe

1. Assess whether you need (or are required to obtain) renter's insurance. Many apartment managers and landlords require that you obtain some level of renter's insurance in order to live on their property, so you may not have a choice in the matter. If you do have the choice, assess whether you'd comfortably be able to replace the value of your possessions if they were suddenly lost, and how likely bodily injury or property damage (caused by you or guests) is to happen in your rented property. If you barely own anything and never have large gatherings, maybe you opt to forgo renter's insurance, but it's so cheap that you should at least consider it (I pay $12 per month for mine).
2. Research and compare insurance providers. If your apartment manager or landlord requires that you obtain a policy, ask them for recommendations (they may require that you get insurance from specific providers).
3. Request quotes from multiple insurance providers. You'll need to provide a copious amount of details about your rented property,

and your personal belongings. Once you receive the quotes, compare factors such as:

   a. Coverage options

   b. Deductibles

   c. Premiums

   d. Any additional benefits or discounts

4. Review the policy terms and conditions before making your final decision. It's important that you're actually able to use your insurance when it's needed, so make sure you read through and fully understand your policy. If any additional hazards, like theft, fire, or flooding, have the potential to happen, ensure they're covered in the policy before finalizing it.

   a. Note: You may receive discounts if you bundle your renter's insurance with another type of insurance offered by the same insurance company, such as auto insurance.

5. Finalize your renter's insurance policy. Request a "proof of insurance" document if renter's insurance is required by your apartment manager or landlord.

6. As a precaution, record a video walking through your entire property that shows all of your possessions. If you ever need to file a claim for lost/damaged property, this will make the process much simpler.

7. Review and update your renter's insurance policy as your living situation changes.

Recap

1. Assess whether you need or are required to get renter's insurance.

2. Research insurance providers. Ask your apartment manager or landlord if there are specific insurance providers they want you to use.

3. Request and compare quotes from multiple insurance providers.

4. Understand your chosen policy, and ensure it includes coverage for theft, fire, and/or flooding if you think these may be a potential issue.

5. Finalize your renter's insurance policy and obtain a "proof of insurance" document that you can present to your apartment manager or landlord (if needed).
6. As a precaution, record a video walking through your entire property that shows all of your possessions. If you ever need to file a claim for lost/damaged property, this will make the process much simpler.
7. Review and update your coverage as your situation changes.

12.6 How to Obtain and Save Money on Car Insurance

Setup Time	Maintenance Time	Function
1 Hour	30 Minutes per Year	Protect Your Money

When watching TV, streaming services, or even scrolling on social media, it's hard not to come across an ad for car insurance. Why? Because it's legally required in every US state except for New Hampshire (which requires you pass a financial responsibility test if you choose to forgo car insurance) (https://www.progressive .com/answers/state-car-insurance-information/#:~:text=New%20 Hampshire%20is%20the%20only,event%20they%20cause%20an%20 accident), and nearly 92% of US households owned at least one vehicle as of 2021 (https://www.forbes.com/advisor/car-insurance/car-ownership-statistics/#:~:text=the%20data%20Embed-,How%20 Many%20Americans%20Own%20a%20Car%3F,up%20from%20 91.2%25%20in%202017). This means you're extremely likely to own a car now or in the future, and it's almost certain that you'll be required to obtain car insurance for it. This recipe will walk you through how to obtain car insurance and potentially save a dollar or two along the way.

Essential Terminology

Car Insurance: A type of insurance that provides coverage for your car and car-related incidents. It's required to have if you own a vehicle in all but one US state. Each state has its own minimum coverage requirements, but common coverages include liability, collision, comprehensive, personal injury, uninsured/underinsured motorist, medical expenses, property damage, rental car, and towing.

Liability Coverage: Helps pay for damages you cause to others in a car accident. It includes coverage for both bodily injury and property damage.

Collision Coverage: Helps pay for damage to your own car if it's damaged or destroyed in a collision with another vehicle or object, regardless of who is at fault (liability coverage covers damage you cause to another party's car in an accident).

Comprehensive Coverage: Helps pay for damage to your car that isn't caused by a collision, which could include vandalism, theft, fire, falling objects, and severe weather.

Personal Injury Protection (PIP): Covers medical expenses, lost wages, and other related costs for you (and any passengers) involved in an accident, regardless of which driver was at fault.

Uninsured/Underinsured Motorist Coverage: As its name implies, it covers your medical expenses and damages if you're involved in an accident with someone who doesn't have insurance or is underinsured.

Medical Payments Coverage: Another straightforward coverage, it helps pay for medical expenses resulting from an accident, regardless of who is at fault.

Property Damage Coverage: Helps pay for damage you cause to someone else's property, like their car, fence, or building.

Rental Car Coverage: Helps pay for the cost of renting a vehicle while your personal vehicle is being repaired due to a covered claim.

Towing and Labor Coverage: Helps pay for emergency roadside assistance and towing expenses if your car breaks down or needs assistance on the road.

Deductible: The amount you're responsible for paying with your own money before insurance coverage kicks in.

Premium: The cost you pay for your insurance coverage, usually on a monthly, bi-annual, or annual basis.

Ingredient List

Required:

- Driver's license
- Vehicle information (make, model, color, VIN, and license plate number)
- Personal information

Recipe

1. Familiarize yourself with your state's coverage requirements (a quick web search will do the trick) and all the additional coverage options (listed under the essential terminology section).
2. Research insurance providers to find the best coverage options and rates for your situation. There are many online comparison tools you can utilize that allow you to compare quotes from multiple insurance companies based on your specific needs. The main factors to consider are coverage options, deductibles, price, and customer reviews. Major car insurance providers include (listed in no specific order):
   a. Allstate
   b. Farmers
   c. GEICO
   d. Nationwide
   e. Progressive
   f. State Farm
   g. USAA

3. Once you've narrowed down your list of providers to two or three companies, contact them directly to ask for quotes based on your specific requirements and vehicle. Again, compare coverage options, premiums, and deductibles among the quotes.

4. Don't be afraid to ask for discounts. Many insurance providers offer discounts for things like good driving records, bundling your car insurance with another policy offered by them like renter's or homeowner's insurance, completing a defensive driving course, or even showing them a transcript of your good grades if you're a student.

   a. Another popular way to receive a discount when you renew your policy is to allow your insurance company to track your driving habits via either a mobile app or a device that they place in your car. This can feel a little invasive, but if you really are a safe and/or infrequent driver, it can meaningfully lower your premium. Data is only collected for a set period of time, so you don't need to worry about them tracking you forever. Also, obviously, if you display bad driving habits (speeding, looking at your phone, suddenly braking), your premium may increase.

5. Choose the policy that looks like the best fit for you, and thoroughly review your coverage options and the terms of your policy.

   a. This sounds silly, but I just realized a week ago (as I'm writing this) that my car insurance didn't include collision or comprehensive coverage. How did I find out, you may ask. It wasn't because I got into an accident: it was because someone tried (and thankfully failed) to break into/steal my car. I obviously wasn't too happy when I walked out to my car and discovered that my driver's door handle and keyhole were badly damaged, but I figured my car insurance would help cover the repair cost. I submitted a claim, and . . . they got back to me saying I was on my own since I didn't have comprehensive coverage. Ironically, instances like this are exactly why I'm writing this book.

When I originally signed up for car insurance, I had *no idea* what any of the coverages meant or what I should sign up for. A resource like this book would've really helped me out.

6. Accept your policy, and ensure you have access to proof of insurance in case you ever get pulled over by the police. These days, you can provide proof of insurance on your phone in most states (either via your insurer's app or a downloaded insurance card), or you could go old school and print off a physical copy that you keep in your glove box.

7. Continue to maintain good driving habits. Accidents and traffic violations could increase the price of your premiums.

8. Review and update your insurance policy, as needed. Rates change over time, so it's important to occasionally compare your rates with those offered by competitors. It's also important to review and update your coverages if you, like a certain personal finance author, didn't exactly have the best idea of what you were signing up for initially.

Recap

1. Familiarize yourself with your state's car insurance coverage requirements, and review all the different types of available coverages.

2. Research and compare quotes from different car insurance providers based on factors like coverage options, deductibles, and premiums.

3. Don't be afraid to ask for, or seek out, discounts.

4. Thoroughly review your chosen policy to ensure you don't run into any surprises if/when you eventually file a claim (like I did when I realized I'm on my own if my car gets vandalized).

5. Continue to maintain good driving habits. Accidents and traffic violations could increase the price of your premiums.

6. Review and update your insurance policy, as needed. Rates change over time, so it's important to occasionally compare your rates with those offered by competitors.

12.7   How to Determine When You Need Life Insurance

Setup Time	Maintenance Time	Function
20 Minutes	N/A	Protect Your Family

Since I create personal finance content on social media, the occasional life insurance salesman tends to show up on my feed shouting stuff like "LIFE INSURANCE IS HOW YOU GET RICH," "LIFE INSURANCE CAN BUILD YOU MORE WEALTH THAN A 401(K)," "LITERALLY EVERY OTHER FINANCIAL PRODUCT IS A BETTER INVESTMENT THAN LIFE INSURANCE BUT THAT WON'T STOP ME FROM TRYING TO SELL IT TO YOU!" Alright, that last one *may* not be something these salesmen say, but it's the closest thing to the truth on that list. If life insurance is such a good "investment," why does it need an army of salespeople to convince you to buy it? Where are all the salesmen trying to get people to open 401(k)s and invest in passive index funds? All jokes aside, life insurance can be a valuable part of your financial toolkit when used appropriately. This recipe will help you find out when that appropriate time is for you.

Essential Terminology

Life Insurance: A contract between you (the "policyholder") and an insurance company. You pay premiums, and in return, the insurance company provides a death benefit to the policy's beneficiaries upon your death.

Beneficiaries: Individuals (or entities) designated to receive the death benefit from a life insurance policy. Beneficiaries typically include your spouse and/or kids.

Death Benefit: The amount of money paid out to the beneficiaries of a life insurance policy when the policyholder passes away.

It's intended to help cover expenses, like funeral costs, and replace the income of the deceased for a period of time.

Premiums: Monthly payments you make to your life insurance provider to maintain your life insurance policy.

Term Life Insurance: Life insurance coverage that covers a specific amount of time, or "term." The term is typically ten, twenty, or thirty years. A death benefit is only paid if the policyholder dies during the term. Term policies typically have the lowest monthly premiums for the most amount of coverage.

Whole Life Insurance: Life insurance that provides lifelong coverage and includes a savings component called "cash value," which can grow over time and be used for loans or withdrawals. This is typically the most expensive form of life insurance.

Indexed Universal Life Insurance: Life insurance that combines a death benefit with the potential for growth based on the performance of investments within the account. It usually costs more than term life insurance but less than whole life insurance.

Fiduciary: A person or entity that is legally and ethically responsible for acting in your best interest over their own.

Ingredient List

Required:

• Knowledge of your current financial, and personal, situations

Recipe

1. Assess whether you have any financial dependents. Do you have a spouse, children, or others who would be in financial trouble if you unexpectedly passed away?
   a. If not, you probably don't need life insurance at this point.
2. Take stock of your financial obligations. If you were to pass, would you leave behind debt such as mortgages, credit card debt, or student loans?

3. Estimate the cost of your funeral expenses. Costs vary widely between cremation and traditional funerals/burials; if you want the latter, consider how it will be paid for.
4. Evaluate your emergency fund (Section 1.3). If you were to unexpectedly pass, would it cover the cost of the items described in the previous points?
5. If going through the previous points still has you on the fence about whether or not to explore life insurance options, consult with a fiduciary, fee-only financial planner. Why fee-only? Because they won't make a commission from selling you life insurance products. Even if the hourly fee seems expensive, it's well worth it to get an unbiased opinion on an area that is filled with so many salesmen prioritizing their profits over your financial well-being.

Recap

1. Assess whether anyone (such as a spouse or children) would undergo severe financial hardship if you were to pass away. If not, you probably don't need life insurance yet.
2. If so, consult with a fiduciary, fee-only financial planner to discuss your life insurance options. Everyone's situation is unique, but a common recommendation (from those who aren't incentivized to sell you specific life insurance products) is to buy term life insurance that covers the time when your children are financially dependent on you, then let the policy lapse once they're on their own.

Chapter 13

Passive Income

13.1 Why Passive Income Is the Best Form of Income

Setup Time	Maintenance Time	Function
N/A	N/A	Make Money

Do you always want to work hard for your money? Or would you rather put your money to work for you and potentially have it generate more income than you earn working? Not only that but would you rather be taxed less on this income your money earns for you? That's what passive income can provide you, but it takes time and effort to get the ball rolling here. This recipe will detail all the reasons passive income is awesome, and this chapter as a whole will walk you through different strategies you can use to earn passive income.

Essential Terminology

Passive Income: Also known as "mailbox money," passive income is money that you earn without actively working for it. It comes from investments, rental properties, or businesses that keep generating money even when you're not putting in a lot (or any) effort. By separating your hours worked from your income, it allows you to obtain true financial freedom (see Section 1.6). But wait, there's more! Passive income is also taxed less than actively earned income.

Active Income: Money you earn from a job. To earn it, you trade your time for money.

Ingredient List

Required:

- Strong financial foundation
- Willingness to put in work up front for a long-term reward
- The desire to separate your hours worked from your income

Why Passive Income Is Awesome

1. Financial independence. By separating your time from your money, you no longer need to be tied down to a traditional job. If you generate enough passive income to cover your expenses, you can spend your time however you wish.
2. It's less risky than having a job. If your only source of income comes from working a job, you're one pink slip away from losing 100% of your income. By generating passive income from multiple different sources, such as investments, real estate investing, and businesses, you ensure that all your income won't suddenly be turned off overnight. If it somehow did, that would mean that all the major financial markets would go to zero and never return, which would likely point to us having a lot more to worry about than dollars in a bank account.
3. Potential to scale. As you invest more money into assets that generate passive income, they'll almost certainly generate even more income for you. If you choose to reinvest the income from your passive investments, you'll earn more and more money over time without increasing your effort level.

4. Tax advantages. Active income is almost always taxed more than passive income. Passive income that is classified as a "long-term capital gain" or "qualified dividend" is taxed at a much lower tax bracket than active income, while passive rental income can take advantage of tax rules like "depreciation" to reduce the amount that is subject to taxation.

5. Legacy building. Unless you're a fan of nepotism, it's hard to pass down your job to your children. It's much easier to pass down a stock portfolio, rental properties, or a business that you own outright. This can create true generational wealth in a way that a job never could.

13.2 How to Earn Passive Income from the Stock Market

Setup Time	Maintenance Time	Function
30–60 Minutes	5 Minutes per Month	Make Money

While passive income can be generated by many sources, it's hard to find one as low-effort as investing in the stock market. The up front setup is very low (you just need to open a brokerage account or IRA (see Sections 2.1 and 2.2), and the ongoing maintenance is almost zero (assuming you invest passively). This recipe will walk you through how to earn passive income from the stock market.

Essential Terminology

Dividends: Cash distributions you may receive as the owner of certain stocks or funds. Dividends can be reinvested into the stocks or funds that paid them, or they can be withdrawn as cash.

Capital Appreciation: The increase in the value of your investments over time. The stock market isn't guaranteed to increase in value in the future, but it historically has due to a combination of improved company performance, technological innovation, and inflation.

Brokerage Account: A non-retirement account that allows you to invest in stocks, bonds, index funds, ETFs, mutual funds, certificates of deposit, etc. There are no contribution, withdrawal, or income limits. Unlike retirement accounts, brokerage accounts do not offer tax-saving incentives for the money you deposit into them. They are free to open and don't have any ongoing account fees (at most major brokers).

Broker: It's a fancy way to refer to the company that hosts your brokerage account. Just as you associate "banks" like Chase, Wells Fargo, and Bank of America with checking accounts, you can associate "brokers" like Fidelity, Vanguard, and Charles Schwab with brokerage accounts. Brokers are specifically licensed to facilitate transactions on the stock market, whereas most "regular" banks aren't.

Index Funds: A "basket" of hundreds, or sometimes thousands, of stocks that you can invest in very similarly to a stock. They aim to passively track the performance of a stock market "index," like the S&P 500 (a group of 500 of the largest US-based companies) or the total stock market.

Mutual Funds: Similar to index funds, but instead of passively tracking an index of stocks, they are controlled by professional investment managers who try to provide outsized returns.

Passive Income: Also known as "mailbox money," passive income is money that you earn without actively working for it. It comes from investments, rental properties, or businesses that keep generating money even when you're not putting in a lot (or any) effort. By separating your hours worked from your income, it allows you to obtain true financial freedom (see Section 1.6). But wait, there's more! Passive income is also taxed less than actively earned income.

Active Income: Money you earn from a job. To earn it, you trade your time for money.

Ingredient List

Required:

- Computer or smartphone
- Brokerage account or IRA (see Sections 2.1 and 2.2)
- Income that you can set aside consistently to invest

Recipe

1. Use Chapter 2 to open a brokerage account or IRA and understand the fundamentals of investing. Be aware that there are two forms of income you can earn through investing in the stock market: capital appreciation and dividends.
2. Determine your investing strategy. If you want investing to be as passive as possible, you may want to consider passively managed, low-fee index funds that track a broad market index. This will allow you to passively track the overall returns of the stock market, which may give you better returns than actively trying to beat the stock market would give you anyway (https://mba .tuck.dartmouth.edu/bespeneckbo/default/AFA611-Eckbo%20 web%20site/AFA611-S8C-FamaFrench-LuckvSkill-JF10.pdf), while also passively being sent dividend payments.
   a. Also, consider which accounts you invest inside of. The tax advantages of accounts like IRAs are phenomenal, but (in most cases) you'll be restricted from withdrawing this money until you reach retirement age. Brokerage accounts, on the other hand, don't have nearly as many tax benefits but you can access this money at will.
3. Ensure you build a diversified portfolio. This means that your investments are spread out among many different stocks and industries, which lowers the overall risk of your investment portfolio. Index funds and mutual funds typically hold a diverse group of stocks inside of them already, reducing the need to do much additional diversification.

4. Decide what to do with your dividends. Dividends can either be taken as cash or automatically reinvested back into the stocks and funds that paid them. If your portfolio is in the growth stage, it typically makes sense to reinvest them. (This is an option you can select on your accounts with most major brokers.) If you reach a point where you could cover a meaningful portion of your living expenses with your dividends, you may want to consider taking them as cash.

5. Be aware of applicable taxes. Section 9.3 details how investments are taxed, but at a high level you need to understand two things: Dividends paid into your brokerage account are always taxed (regardless of whether you reinvest them), and you'll also be taxed if you sell a stock, index fund, or other investment for a higher price than you bought it for. If your dividends start to generate a significant tax liability, you may want to hold a portion of them in cash so you're prepared to pay this when you file your tax return.

6. Play the long game. The best way to lose money in the stock market is to try to get rich quickly. The stock market won't replace your day job income overnight; it'll likely take decades. Patiently invest a set percentage of your income in the stock market month over month, let compound interest do the trick, and you'll be sitting pretty in the next ten to twenty years. It takes money to make money in the stock market. The best way to increase your returns is to invest more money (for example, a 10% return on an account with $10,000 invested is $1,000, while it's $100,000 on an account with $1 million invested), so focus your time and energy earning more money at your day job or side hustle.

Recap

1. Read Chapter 2 to learn how to open investing accounts.
2. Determine a passive investing strategy to follow.
3. Ensure your portfolio is diversified to reduce overall risk.
4. Decide whether or not to reinvest your dividends.
5. Be aware of, and plan for, taxes on your dividends and capital gains.

6. Play the long game. Don't try to get rich quickly. Invest as much as you can and let compound interest work its magic over the years.

13.3   How to Earn Passive Income from Real Estate Investing

Setup Time	Maintenance Time	Function
Many Hours	Various, but Can Be Extensive	Make Money

While investing in the stock market (Section 13.2) may be the most passive form of passive income, real estate investing has the potential to replace your day job's income much more quickly. However, it also comes with more risk and a much larger time commitment (especially up front). This recipe will walk you through how to earn passive income from real estate investing.

Essential Terminology

Passive Income: Also known as "mailbox money," passive income is money that you earn without actively working for it. It comes from investments, rental properties, or businesses that keep generating money even when you're not putting in a lot (or any) effort. By separating your hours worked from your income, it allows you to obtain true financial freedom (see Section 1.6). But wait, there's more! Passive income is also taxed less than actively earned income.

Active Income: Money you earn from a job. To earn it, you trade your time for money.

Real Estate Investing: When you buy properties, like houses or buildings, with the goal of making money from them. Real estate investors can earn monthly income through rent, appreciation from property improvements, and unique tax advantages that can reduce their taxable income.

Property Manager: A person or company who oversees rental properties on the owner's behalf. They handle tasks like finding tenants, collecting rent, maintaining the property, and cleaning the property. Hiring a property manager makes real estate investing much more passive, though it's not cheap.

Long-Term Rental Strategy: When a property is leased out to a tenant for a long period of time, generally one or more years. This generates a stable source of income for the landlord, but it has the lowest income potential of the three main rental strategies.

Mid-Term Rental Strategy: When a property is rented out to tenants for a moderate duration, usually ranging from a few weeks to a few months. These are typically furnished rentals (so you'd have to pay for furniture) provided to those who are traveling to the area for temporary work (like traveling nurses) or extended vacations. Landlords are able to charge more rent than long-term rentals for these shorter stays but must deal with an increased rate of tenant turnover.

Short-Term Rental Strategy: When a property is rented out for a short duration, ranging from a per-night basis to stays of a couple of weeks. This essentially turns your property into a hotel, meaning you'll need to put extra effort into furnishing, amenities, and cleaning services. These rentals are most popular among vacationers and travelers, so demand can fluctuate heavily based on seasonality. This strategy faces the most restrictions from city councils (they're banned or limited in many areas), so it's important to check the regulations of the area you want to invest in before looking for short-term rental properties. Because of the additional effort required to run a short-term rental, they also have the highest income potential of any of the three main rental strategies.

Real Estate Syndications: When investors pool their resources together to collectively invest in a large real estate project, like an apartment complex or self-storage facility. The project is actively managed by a "general partner," while the "limited partners" are passive investors who receive a share of the profits from the deal based on their investment amount. Limited partners are usually required to contribute a minimum investment of somewhere in the neighborhood of tens of thousands of dollars, so this isn't an investment strategy with a low barrier to entry.

Down Payment: The initial cash lump sum you need to pay when buying a house. "Standard" down payments equal 20% of a home's purchase price, though first-time homebuyers can put as little as 3.5% down if they qualify for an FHA loan.

Mortgage: A loan to buy a house; the house itself serves as collateral for the loan. This means, if you fail to make your loan payments, the bank that issued your mortgage could potentially take ownership of your home.

Closing Costs: Fees and expenses that must be paid to the different parties in a real estate transaction when buying a home. Closing costs can include lender fees, appraisal costs, title insurance, and real estate agent fees.

Credit Score: A number that tells the bank how trustworthy a person is when it comes to borrowing money; think of it as your financial report card. Credit scores range from 300 on the low end to 850 being perfect: 650 to 700 is considered fair, 700 to 750 is considered good, and anything over 750 is considered excellent.

Emergency Fund: A sum of cash set aside for unexpected financial needs or emergencies, like medical expenses or car repairs. It provides a safety net, allowing you to handle unforeseen circumstances without having to borrow money or rely on credit cards. The general recommendation is to have between three and six months' worth of necessary expenses held in your emergency fund.

Ingredient List

Required:

- A solid financial foundation
- Savings needed to buy a property
- Emergency fund for the property
- Willingness to become a landlord

Recipe

1. Determine your investment strategy. Offering long-term rentals provides the most stability but the lowest profit potential. Short-term rentals require the most work and have the highest

level of uncertainty, but also have the highest profit potential. Mid-term rentals fall in between those two, but you'd need to ensure there's demand for mid-term rentals in your area since it's a less common choice for renters. If actively investing in real estate doesn't sound appealing to you, but you have the ability to invest mid-five figures, you may want to consider investing in a real estate syndication.

2. Educate yourself heavily on the strategy you've chosen. Learn as much as you can from books, videos, and even mentors before you start investing. It's impossible to know all the ins and outs before you start investing, but learning a couple of tips from someone who has been through this process many times could save you from a meaningful number of headaches.

3. Build your financial foundation. As you can see in Section 7.3, buying a house can be *expensive*. From down payments to closing costs to insurance to your mortgage, there's a seemingly endless amount of costs you'll incur just during the home-buying process, let alone the repairs and maintenance (and potentially furnishing) you'll need to cover once you own the property. Save up more cash than you think you'll need for the down payment and closing costs, save up an emergency fund to cover any of the unexpected expenses of home ownership, and ensure your credit score is in tip-top shape so you qualify for as low of an interest rate on your mortgage as possible. Money doesn't grow on trees, but also try to make sure you don't buy a property that you'd struggle to cover the mortgage of on your own if it sits vacant for longer than you'd hope.

4. Connect with a real estate agent and mortgage lender that primarily work with real estate investors in your chosen niche. Your real estate agent will help you find a property that fits your criteria in an area where there will be rental demand for your chosen niche, while your lender will work with you to get the best loan for your situation (get quotes from multiple mortgage lenders to ensure you get the best rates possible).

5. With the help of your real estate agent, evaluate potential investment properties in your target market based on criteria like

property location, condition, potential rental income, expenses (insurance, property taxes, utilities, HOA, etc.), and the rental regulations of the city it's located in.

   a. This is the hard part of real estate investing: if good deals were easy to find, everyone would be a real estate investor. Don't be surprised if it takes months to find a property that makes sense for you, and be even less surprised when someone outbids you for that property. That's how these things work. You just need to keep getting up to bat and, eventually, you'll find a property that works for you.

6. Acquire and manage your properties. Once you acquire a property, start working on any necessary rehab/updates and get the place ready to be rented out. Additional work could include furnishing the property and hiring a cleaning team if you're implementing a short or mid-term rental strategy. Hire a professional real estate photographer to capture beautiful pictures of your property and post them along with your listings on websites like Zillow, apartments.com, and Airbnb. Once the upfront work is done and tenant/guest management systems are put in place, you'll likely only need to commit a couple of hours (or less) per week to managing your properties.

   a. If you don't want to deal with the weekly responsibilities of being a landlord (tenant communication, property maintenance, and coordinating cleanings), you could consider hiring a property manager. This is what truly turns real estate into a passive investment, though it's not cheap.

7. Earn passive income through property appreciation, rental income, and tax benefits. Though real estate is less passive than investing in the stock market (Section 13.2), it's still *way* more passive than working 40 hours per week at a job. However, because you're collecting monthly rent, real estate investing has the potential to replace the income from your day job in a matter of years, if done correctly, compared to the decades it'd likely take in the stock market.

8. Expand your portfolio. You've bought one property; time to do it again if you want to increase your total cash flow.

Recap

1. Determine your real estate investing strategy. Are you okay with lower cash flow in exchange for the passiveness of offering long-term rentals? Or would you be happy to put in more work for the additional return potential of short-term rentals?
2. Educate yourself heavily on your chosen strategy.
3. Real estate is expensive and has many hidden costs; build a strong financial foundation before investing in it.
4. Connect with a real estate agent and request quotes from multiple lenders who primarily work with real estate investors.
5. The hard part of real estate investing is finding a property that fits your investing criteria. Factors to consider are property location, condition, potential rental income, expenses (insurance, property taxes, utilities, HOA, etc.), and the rental regulations of the city it's located in.
6. Acquire and manage your property. Get it rent-ready and fill it with tenants/guests. Outsource to a property manager to make it as passive of an investment as possible.
7. Earn (mostly) passive income through property appreciation, rental income, and tax benefits.
8. Expand your rental property portfolio to increase your cash flow.

13.4   How to Earn Passive Income from Digital Products

Setup Time	Maintenance Time	Function
Many Hours	Varies	Make Money

If investing in physical real estate (Section 13.3) doesn't seem like it's in your wheelhouse, you could try profiting off of digital real estate. No, I'm not talking about speculating on land in the metaverse (remember that craziness?); I'm talking about creating and selling digital products online. You can package your unique knowledge, skills, and expertise into an information product like an e-book, online course, or software, and sell it to an audience who has been searching for exactly what you're providing. This recipe will show you how to make passive income from the "build once, sell twice" potential digital products offer.

Essential Terminology

Digital Products: Information products you spend time up front building, but can then be sold an unlimited number of times on the internet at no additional cost to you. Examples include e-books, templates, online courses, graphics, music, and software.

Passive Income: Also known as "mailbox money," passive income is money that you earn without actively working for it. It comes from investments, rental properties, or businesses that keep generating money even when you're not putting in a lot (or any) effort. By separating your hours worked from your income, it allows you to obtain true financial freedom (see Section 1.6). But wait, there's more! Passive income is also taxed less than actively earned income.

Active Income: Money you earn from a job. To earn it, you trade your time for money.

Ingredient List

Required:

- Computer or smartphone
- Valuable expertise, knowledge, and/or skills

Optional:

- Existing online audience (helps get initial customers for your product)

Recipe

1. Determine your unique expertise, knowledge, and/or skills. If someone came up to you and asked you to teach them about one topic for the next hour, what's the one thing you can speak about confidently for a full hour? Is it cooking? Baking? Playing an instrument? Hitting a golf ball? Digital performance marketing? There are billions of people in the world; chances are some of them are interested in learning/improving on something you're already an expert in.

   a. If you're not necessarily an expert on any specific topic, think of different ways you can make someone's life easier when using software/programs that you use on a daily basis. For example, you could sell productivity templates for people to use on a platform like Notion.

2. Imagine your ideal customer. Who exactly are you trying to sell your product to? Age, gender, interests, job title, income level—be as specific as possible. The more you define your ideal customer, the better you'll be able to serve (and market toward) them.

3. Decide on the format of your digital product. Will it be an online course? Will it be an e-book? Will it be a template? This will determine where you sell your product.

4. Speaking of where to sell your product, choose a hosting platform for your product. If you're selling an e-book, you might want to use a self-publishing service like Amazon Kindle Direct Publishing. If you're selling an online course, you might want to use a platform like Kajabi or Gumroad.

   a. Kajabi is my favorite platform for creating and hosting digital products; use my link to get an extended free trial: nicktalksmoney.com/kajabi.

5. Create your digital product. Kajabi is how I make and host my online courses, Canva is how I create templates and graphics (nicktalksmoney.com/canva), or, if you're writing an e-book, you could use a free tool like Google Docs.

6. Determine your price point. This is a delicate balancing act, as you want to price it high enough to seem like a valuable product,

but you don't want to outprice your core buyers. From personal experience, I'd suggest starting at the lower end of your price spectrum and increasing it after your initial wave of students pass through the course and leave positive feedback you can share on the sales page.

7. Develop a marketing strategy. Will you try to get eyeballs on your product for free by creating social media content around it? Will you pay to use something like Meta ads to promote your product directly in front of your target customer base? Or will you pay influencers to make content promoting your digital product?

8. Automate as much as possible. Integrate payment providers, like Stripe and PayPal, to make the checkout process as easy as possible. Run automated email marketing sequences for new people who sign up to your email list. The hosting platform you use should automatically deliver the customer the digital product after they pay for it.

9. Optimize and update your content. As you receive feedback from students, update your product to include the features they request. Also ensure to update it based on any overarching market trends, like AI currently is at the time of writing this book, as it could expose your product to a whole new set of potential customers.

10. Earn (mostly) passive income. Once the product is completed, your only real time commitment is marketing, which can be mostly automated if you use something like Meta ads or outsource your promotional posts to social media influencers.

11. If successful, consider expanding your digital product library. If someone bought and enjoyed your original digital product, why wouldn't they want to buy the next product you come out with?

Recap

1. Determine your unique expertise, knowledge, and/or skills. This is what you'll build your digital product around.

2. Clearly picture your ideal customer. This will help you craft your product and marketing strategy.

3. Decide on the format for your digital product. How would some-one be most likely to consume the information you're providing?

4. Choose a hosting platform for your product. I recommend using Kajabi (nicktalksmoney.com/kajabi) to host most forms of digi-tal products.

5. Determine your price point. Make it high enough to appear valuable, but not so high that it restricts your ideal customers from purchasing it.

6. Developing a marketing strategy. Creating content yourself, paying others to create promotional content, or using Meta Ads are all viable options.

7. Automate as much as possible.

8. Optimize and update your content as you receive feedback from students.

9. Sit back and earn (mostly) passive income. All you need to worry about at this point is marketing.

10. If successful, expand your digital product library.

13.5   How to Earn Passive Income from Affiliate Marketing

Setup Time	Maintenance Time	Function
Many Hours	Varies	Make Money

If you got excited about the prospect of the unlimited potential of selling online we discussed in Section 13.4, but you don't want to/can't think of a product you want to create, affiliate marketing could be a path for you to consider. Instead of creating and selling their own products, affiliate marketers promote existing products from different companies and earn commissions based on how many sales they generate. After a setup period where you're learning the ropes, you could create a passive income stream using affiliate marketing that requires little upkeep from you. That's what this recipe will teach you to do.

Essential Terminology

Affiliate Marketing: A performance-based marketing strategy where you promote existing products or services and earn a commission for each sale you generate. It's a true eat-what-you-kill side hustle. Affiliates are provided a unique tracking link, which they then create content around and post across blogs, social media, and anywhere else they think they might get eyeballs from.

Affiliate Network: A platform that connects affiliate marketers with affiliate programs. They also handle the analytics tracking and payouts for affiliate programs, while serving as a hub for the affiliate marketer to manage their affiliate relationships.

Affiliate Program: A program offered by companies that allows people to become affiliates for them and receive a commission in exchange for driving sales to their product or service.

Digital Products: Information products you spend time up front building, but can then be sold an unlimited number of times on the internet at no additional cost to you. Examples include e-books, templates, online courses, graphics, music, and software.

Passive Income: Also known as "mailbox money," passive income is money that you earn without actively working for it. It comes from investments, rental properties, or businesses that keep generating money even when you're not putting in a lot (or any) effort. By separating your hours worked from your income, it allows you to obtain true financial freedom (see Section 1.6). But wait, there's more! Passive income is also taxed less than actively earned income.

Active Income: Money you earn from a job. To earn it, you trade your time for money.

Ingredient List

Required:

- Computer (recommended) or smartphone
- Platform(s) or website(s) (social media account, website, blog, etc.)
  - My favorite website hosting platform is Kajabi; sign up for an extended free trial at: nicktalksmoney.com/kajabi.

Recipe

1. Select a niche. In order to attract eyeballs to your affiliate links, you need to create content targeted at a specific niche. Ideally, this will be a niche that you have some level of expertise and/or experience in. Your affiliate links will center around this niche.
   a. You don't need to choose a single niche; you can create multiple websites/social media accounts for different niches. For example, you could have different websites for fitness, gaming, and cooking.
2. Research and apply for affiliate networks. I'm part of three affiliate networks that give me access to a wide array of affiliate programs. These networks are Impact Radius, ShareASale, and Amazon Associates. Between these three affiliate networks, you should get access to affiliate programs in basically any major niche.
3. Join affiliate programs. On Impact Radius and ShareASale, you're allowed to browse and apply for affiliate programs that interest you. If you're part of Amazon Associates, you can create affiliate links for products sold on Amazon. Choose affiliate programs and/or products that fit in the niche of content that you plan to create.
4. Create quality content. This is the hard part: You need to create content that other people derive value from where you can plug your affiliate links. For example, you could write a blog post about a specific workout program and include affiliate links for the workout app you used along with Amazon affiliate links for any of the workout gear you recommend. Or you can write a book about personal finance and include affiliate links to your favorite financial tools. In order to be an effective affiliate marketer, you can't constantly be promoting junk. Curate your affiliates to only platforms or products that you actually use and enjoy.
5. Share your content through as many channels as possible: social media, email, and other online communities. Share your content wherever you think your target audience lives on the internet.
6. Analyze and optimize. Affiliate programs tend to provide you with a *ton* of analytics, some of the key ones being clicks,

conversions, and earnings generated by your links. If you notice a certain style of content is generating more clicks than others, double down on that style of content. Likewise, if there are certain products that are performing better than others.

7. As you begin to understand the affiliate marketing process, continue to scale. Create more content, in more niches, for more affiliates.

8. As your content begins to gain more and more organic viewership, affiliate marketing becomes a lot more passive. One blog post that you spend two hours writing could be seen by thousands of people over the coming years, so while you'll need to generate content on a fairly consistent basis to generate income from affiliate marketing, the internet ensures the time you do spend working is very highly leveraged.

Recap

1. Choose a niche to create your initial content around. Ensure it's a niche you have some level of expertise in and it's one that has a good selection of affiliate programs.

2. Join affiliate networks to browse large conglomerations of affiliate programs. I'm part of Impact Radius, ShareASale, and Amazon Associates.

3. Join affiliate programs that make sense for your niche. Ensure you can organically mention them in your content.

4. Create high-quality content about your niche. Insert affiliate links wherever appropriate (be sure not to overdo it or recommend products that the customer will have a bad experience with).

5. Share your content in as many places as possible.

6. Analyze and optimize your content.

7. As you begin to have success, expand your affiliate marketing endeavors.

8. While it's hard to make this fully passive, your content can continue to get organic views for years after you post it. This means, after building up a library of quality content, you could be generating meaningful income for years with no additional work.

Index

4% rule
  creation, 14
  term, 13, 181
20/4/10 rule, term, 79
50/30/20 rule, term, 8
401(k) match, term, 27–28, 136
401(k) plans, 26, 162, 163, 178
  contribution amount,
    decision, 28
  monitoring/analyzing, 29
  mutual funds mix, 29
  opening, 27–29
  rollover, 183–186
  term, 27, 135, 176,
    180, 183–184
403(b) plan, 27, 178
457(b) plans, 178
529 Education Savings Plan,
  investment, 106

529 plan
  age-based target date fund,
    usage, 107
  research/comparison, 106
  term, 105
  usage, 105–108
529 Prepaid Tuition Plan,
  avoidance, 106

A
Academics, approach
  (seriousness), 94
Account rollover, term, 30
Active income, term, 226, 228,
  231, 237, 241
Advanced Placement (AP) classes
  enrollment, 94
  term, 92
Affiliate marketing, term, 241

Affiliate network
  research/application, 242
  term, 241
Affiliate program
  joining, 242
  term, 241
Age-based target date fund,
    usage, 107
Amended tax term
  documentation, gathering, 171
  function/filing, 168–172
  term, 166, 169
Assets
  investment, term, 66
  transfer, term, 30
  types, pros/cons, 32–36
Authorized user, term, 57, 92
Avalanche method, 71–73

B
Bad debt
  good debt, differentiation,
    65–67
  term, 66
Bank
  research/selection, 2
  term, 1
Bank of America, 20, 24, 30, 39,
    161, 184, 192, 198, 228
Beneficiaries, term, 221
Big 3 brokers, 21
Bonds, 19
  pros/cons, 35–36
Brokerage account
  term, 19–20, 161, 228
  usage/opening, 36, 229
Brokers
  change, 29–32

contact, 31
  mobile-first brokers (investing
    apps), 21–22
  paperwork, transfer, 31
  selection, 22, 26
  term, 20, 24–25, 30, 39, 161,
    184, 192, 198–199, 228
Budget, following, 9
Budgeting, 8–9
  in-depth examination, 9
Bulletproof budget
  building, 7–10
  red flags, 9
Business
  expenses, over-reporting (IRS
    attention), 158
  owner, tax payments, 154–160
  plan/roadmap, creation,
    144–145

C
Capital appreciation,
    term, 227–228
Capital gains
  tax, understanding, 163
  term, 161, 191–192
Capital losses, term, 161
Career advancement, 141–142
Car insurance
  discounts, request, 219
  obtaining/money saving,
    216–220
  policy, selection/acceptance,
    219–220
  providers, research, 218
  term, 217
Car purchases
  advice, 79–82

decision, 82–85
financing, pre-approval, 80
upfront costs, 84
Cars
high-pressure sales tactics,
disengagement, 81
leasing, decision, 82–85
loans, term, 67
ownership, 83
research, 80
warranty coverage, 84
Certificates of deposit (CDs), 19
Charitable donations
tax return reporting, 187–190
term, 188
Charitable giving, 187
Charitable organizations, eligibility
(determination), 189
Charles Schwab, 20, 24, 30,
39, 161, 184, 192, 194,
198–199, 228
Chase, 20, 24, 30, 39, 161, 184,
192, 198, 228
Checking account
opening, 1–2
payment card, link, 43
term, 1
Children
credit score, building, 56–58
investments, 39–41
Closing costs
saving, 119
term, 118, 124, 233
College
529 plan, 105–108
bachelor's degree, cost, 91
costs, 101
grants

application, 95–98
maximization, 103
term, 96, 102
in-state public university,
cost, 91
investment, approach, 101–105
money, saving, 91–95
scholarships, application,
98–101
selection, 102–103
College in Schools (CIS)
classes, enrollment, 94
term, 92
Collision coverage, term, 217
Comprehensive cover-
age, term, 217
Concurrent enrollment program,
term, 92–93
Consolidated 1099, 152, 157, 163
Consumer debt, term, 66–67
Contribution limit, term, 24
Copayments (copays),
term, 202, 206
Corrected tax documents,
term, 170
Cost basis, term, 161
Credit, 43
mix, 55
report, term, 54
utilization, 55
control, 58
Credit card
application, 61
autopay, usage, 47, 55
benefits, maximization, 62
opening, 47–53
pros/cons, 45–46
research/comparison, 52–53

Credit card (*continued*)
  signup bonus, 86
    spending requirements,
      meeting, 61–62, 63
    term, 60
  term, 43–44, 48, 51, 60
  usage, decision, 43
Credit card rewards
  points, accumulation, 62
  redemption, 63
  term, 59
  usage, 59–63
Credit-optimized method, 46
Credit score
  building, 54–56, 93–94
  calculation, understanding, 55
  checking, 49, 52
  required credit score, term, 75
  term, 44, 48–49, 51–52, 54,
    57, 60, 233
Credit union
  research/selection, 2
  term, 2
Current savings rate,
    adjustment, 17
Custodial account
  account/application, decision/
    submission, 40
  funding plan, creation, 40
  term, 39

D
Death benefit, term, 221–222
Debit card
  pros/cons, 44–45
  term, 43
  usage, decision, 43
Debt, 65

avalanche method, 71–73
  term, 71
balance, payment, 68–69
consolidation, 74–76
  loan, location, 75
  term, 74
good debt, bad debt
    (differentiation), 65–67
listing, 69, 72
payment, 68–70, 73
  money, allocation, 70
payoff rate, 75
snowball method, 68–70
  term, 68–69
term, 65, 68, 71, 74
Debt management plan (DMP)
  enrollment, 77
  qualifying, 76–78
  term, 76
Deductible, term, 201,
    207, 214, 218
Delayed retirement, term, 174
De minimis, term, 151, 156
Depreciation, 84
  term, 83
Digital products
  content, optimization/
    updating, 239
  format, decision, 238
  sale, 238
  term, 237, 241
Direct rollovers, 185
Diversified portfolio,
    building, 229
Dividends
  taxation, preparation, 163
  term, 161–162, 227
  usage, 230

Donations, making, 188
Donor-advised fund (DAF)
  contribution, 194
  investment strategy,
    selection, 194
  monitoring, 195
  opening, 190–195
  provider, selection, 193–194
  term, 190–191
  usage, 193
Down payment
  saving, 119
  term, 83, 114, 118,
    122, 124, 233
Dual credit program, term, 92–93
Dwelling coverage, term, 210

E
Early retirement, term, 174
Emergency fund
  building, 5–7, 88–89
  location, determination, 6
  term, 5–6, 233
Employee benefits
  maximization, 135–139
  package, review, 137
  term, 135
  workshops, attendance, 138
Employee retirement benefits,
    evaluation, 137
Employee stock purchase
    plan (ESPP)
  offering, investigation, 137–138
  term, 136
Employer Identification Number
    (EIN), term, 155
Employer-sponsored health
    insurance, term, 206

Employer-sponsored retirement
    plan (401(k))
  RMD rules, application, 178
  term, 136
Equifax, credit report, 55
Estimated tax payments
  term, 154–155
Exchange-traded funds
    (ETFs), 19
  pros/cons, 35
Expenses, analysis, 182
Experian, credit report, 55
Extended repayment plan, 110
  term, 109

F
FDIC insurance, 2
  term, 4
Federal student loans, term, 66
Fee-only financial planner,
    consultation, 223
FHA loan, qualification, 114,
    122, 124, 233
Fidelity, 20, 24, 30, 39, 161, 184,
    192, 193, 198, 228
Fiduciary, term, 222
Financial accounts, evaluation,
    181
Financial dependents, presence
    (assessment), 222
Financial foundation,
    building, 234
Financial habits, maintenance, 56
Financial independence
    number
  calculation, 12–15
  division, 14
  term, 13, 16, 226

Financial obligations,
    assessment, 222
Flexible spending account
    (FSA), term, 136
Form 1040, 158–159
Form 1040-X
    completion/filing, 171
    term, 169
Form 1098, 152, 158
Form 1098-T, 152, 1580
Form 1099-B, 152, 157, 163
Form 1099-DIV, 152, 153,
    157, 159, 163
Form 1099-INT, 152, 157, 163
Form 1099-MISC, 152, 158
Form 1099-NEC, 157
Form 4858, filing, 167
Form 4868
    completion/submission, 168
    term, 165
Form 8283, completion, 189
Form K-1, term, 166
Form W-2, 152
    term, 150, 155
Form W-4, 151
    term, 150
Form W-9
    submission, 157
    term, 155
Fractional share investing,
    term, 37
Free Application for Federal
    Student Aid (FAFSA)
    completion, 97–98
    term, 96
Freelancer, tax payments,
    154–160
Full Retirement Age (FRA)

    determination, 174
    term, 173–174
Full-time business owner,
    becoming (signs), 147
Funeral expenses, estimation,
    223

G
Good debt
    bad debt, differentiation, 65–67
    term, 66
Grace period, term, 109
Grants
    application, 95–98
    maximization, 103
    search/application, 97
    term, 96, 102
Gumroad, 238

H
Healthcare
    choices, finalization, 204–205
    plan options, comparison, 204
Health insurance
    coverage, selection
        (factors), 209
    marketplace, term, 202
    obtaining, 201–205
    term, 135–136, 201, 206
Health maintenance organiza-
    tions (HMOs), term, 207
Health savings account (HSA)
    eligibility, 199
    term, 207, 136, 197–198,
        202–203
    usage, 197–200, 205–210
High-deductible health
    plan (HDHP)

enrollment, 199
term, 198, 203, 207
High-yield savings account
(HYSAs), 163
opening, 3–5
term, 4, 6
Homeowner's insurance, 210–213
term, 210
House
financial aspect, analysis,
114–115
hacking, 123–127
path/goals, 125
term, 124
property, renovation, 126
purchase, 118–121
quotes, comparison, 212
rent/buy decision, 113–115
rent/mortgage payment,
expense (analysis),
116–117
search, initiation, 125, 211–212
tenants, search/screening, 126
House poor, term, 113–114, 116

I
Income-driven repayment (IDR)
plans, 110
term, 109
Independent contractor, tax
payments, 154–160
Indexed universal life insurance,
term, 222
Index funds, 19
pros/cons, 33–34
term, 228
Indirect rollovers, 185
Individual Retirement Accounts
(IRAs), 162

401(k) rollover, 183–186
opening, 28, 229
self-managed IRA, 30
usage, 236
Inherited Roth IRAs, 178
Insurance, 197
Interest rate
reduction, debt consolidation
(usage), 74–76
term, 75, 122
Interest, term, 69, 72
Internal Revenue Service (IRS)
Free File Program,
term, 150, 155
payment, receiving, 170
term, 149, 154, 160, 165, 169,
177, 187, 191
Internship, 104
term, 102
Investment
apps, 21–22
children, investments, 39–41
funding plan, creation, 40
order type/placement, 38
properties, evaluation, 234–235
selection, 32–36
strategy, determination,
229, 233–234
tax, 160–164
payments/forms, 162–163
Itemized deduction,
term, 188, 191

J
Job
advancement, readiness,
141–142
compensation, discussion, 134
landing, 104

Job (*continued*)
  network, building, 140
  offer, salary negotiation, 130
Job hopping
  term, 139
  usage, 139–142

K
Kajabi, 238

L
Leasing
  buyout option, 85
  ownership equity, absence, 85
  term, 82
Legacy building, 227
Liability coverage, term,
    211, 214, 217
Life insurance
  need, determination, 221–223
  term, 221
Lifestyle factors, analysis, 115
Limited liability company (LLC),
    taxes (professional
    assistance), 156
Limit order, term, 37
Living expenses, reduction,
    123–127
Loan
  amount, term, 75
  pre-approval, 115
Long-term rental strategy,
    term, 232

M
Mailbox money, 231, 237, 241
Major
  selection, 103–104
  term, 102

Market demand, research, 144
Marketing strategy, development,
    239
Market order, term, 327
Medical payments coverage,
    term, 217
Mid-term rental strategy, term, 232
Minimum withdrawal
    age, term, 24
Mobile budgeting app, usage, 11
Mobile-first brokers, 21–22
MOHELA, 110
Monthly budget, creation,
    69, 72–73
Mortgage
  15-year mortgage, 30-year
    mortgage (contrast),
    121–123
  broker, contact (loan
    pre-approval), 115
  definition, 114, 118, 121
  lender, connection, 234
  options, evaluation, 122–123
  pre-approval, 120, 125
  term, 121, 124, 211, 233
Mostly-credit method, 46–47
Mostly-debit method, 46
Mutual funds, 19
  mix, 29
  pros/cons, 34–35
  term, 228

N
National Foundation for
    Credit Counseling
    (NFCC), term, 76
Navient, 110
NCUA Insurance, government
    protection, 2

Nelnet, 110
Network coverage, term, 202, 206
Networking, term, 102
Net worth
    analysis, 12
    calculation, 10–12
    calculator spreadsheet,
        usage, 11
    goal, 14
    term, 11, 13, 16
    tracking, 12
Networthify, usage, 16
Non-charitable itemized deduc-
    tions amounts, total, 189

O
Online-only banks, offerings, 6
On-time payments, making, 46
Open enrollment period
    enrollment, 208–209
    term, 201, 208
Ordinary income tax
    rate, term, 162
Origination fee, term, 75

P
Paid time off (PTO), usage, 138
Passive income, 225–227
    content, creation/sharing, 242
    mailbox money, 231, 237, 241
    scaling, 226
    stream, creation, 240
    tax advantages, 227
    term, 225–226, 228, 231, 237
Passive income, earning
    affiliate marketing,
        impact, 240–243
    digital products,
        impact, 236–240

property appreciation/rental
    income/tax benefits,
        impact, 235
    real estate investing,
        impact, 231–236
    stock market, impact, 227–231
PayPal, usage, 239
Personal injury protection
    (PIP), term, 217
Personal property
    coverage, term, 211
    term, 213
Pets
    cost, 87–91
    emergency fund,
        building, 88–89
    financial commitment, 90
    insurance, 88
    medications, purchases, 90
    puppies/kittens, cost, 88
Portfolio, expansion, 235–236
Post-Secondary Enrollment
    Options (PSEOs)
        offerings, 94–95
        term, 92–93
Pre-approval, term, 118, 124
Preferred provider organization
    (PPO), term, 207
Premiums, term, 202, 206,
    214, 218, 222
Price point, determination,
    238–239
Principal, reduction
    (avoidance), 17
Private student loans, term, 67
Profit and loss statement
    creation, 159
    term, 155
Profit-sharing plans, 178

Promotion, request, 140–141
Proof of insurance,
          obtaining, 212
Property
     acquisition/management, 235
     damage coverage, term, 217
     manager, term, 232
Purchases, 79
     buying, term, 83

Q
Qualified charitable distribution
          (QCD), 179
     term, 177
Qualified charitable
          organization, term, 191
Qualified education
          expenses, term, 105

R
Raise
     request, 133–135, 140–141
     term, 133
Real estate agents
     connection, 234
     search, 120, 125
Real estate syndication, term, 232
Rental car coverage, term, 217
Renter's insurance
     obtaining, 213–216
     policy terms/conditions,
          review, 215
     requirement, assessment, 214
     term, 213
Repayment plan, term, 109
Repayment terms, 75
Required credit score, term, 75
Required minimum
          distributions (RMDs)

automated withdrawals, 179
     penalties/rules, 178
     penalty, term, 177
     term, 177, 181
Retirement, 173
     accounts, drawing
          (requirement), 176–179
     annual spending,
          determination, 180–183
     HSA, usage, 197–200
     options, 174
     savings rate selection, 15–18
Robo advisor, 20, 22
Rollover
     method, 185
     term, 184
Rollover IRA
     holding, 185
     term, 184
Roth IRAs, 107, 163, 179
     contribution eligibility,
          determination, 25
     opening, 23–26
     term, 24, 184

S
Salary
     increase, 129–132
     portion, investment, 176
     raising, 139–142
     range, research, 130
SARSEPs, 178
Savings account, payment, 3–4
Savings goal, setting, 6
Savings rate
     current savings rate,
          adjustment, 17
     selection, 15–18
     term, 15

Schedule C, 158–159
  term, 155
Scholarships
  application, 98–101
  maximization, 103
  search, 100
  term, 99, 101–102
Secured credit card
  research/comparison, 49–50
  term, 48, 51
SEP IRAs, 178
Short-term capital gains, 161
Short-term rental strategy,
      term, 232
Side hustle
  bookkeeping, 146
  business plan/roadmap,
      creation, 144–145
  failure, acceptance, 146
  initiation, 142–148
  market demand, research, 144
  term, 143
Signing bonus
  attention, 131
  negotiation, 129–132
  term, 129
SIMPLE IRAs, 178
SIPC insurance, 20
Snowball
  method, 68–70
    term, 68–69
  repetition/building, 70
Social Security Administration
    (SSA), payments, 180–181
Social Security benefits
  drawing, 173–175
  term, 173, 180–181
Social Security, online account
    (creation), 175

Special enrollment period,
    term, 202, 208
Spending
  accident, 17–18
  automatic tracking, 9
  habits, evaluation, 46
Standard deduction,
    term, 188, 191
Standard repayment plan, 110
    term, 109
Starting salary
  negotiation, 129–132
  term, 129
Stock market investing, 19
Stocks, 194
  purchase, 36–38
  term, 37
Stocks, pros/cons, 32–33
Stripe, usage, 239
Student credit card, research/
    comparison, 49–50
Student loans, payment,
    108–111

T
Take-home income,
    calculation, 117
Tax
  deduction, term, 188, 191, 198
  extensions, 164–168
    determination, 166–167
    term, 165, 170
  filing deadline, term, 155–156,
    165–166, 169–170
  law, changes (awareness), 164
  liability, term, 150,
    156, 166, 170
  payments, 149–160
    understanding, 151

Tax (*continued*)
    refund, term, 150,
        156, 166, 170
    return
        filing, 153, 160
        term, 149, 154, 160–161,
            165, 169, 187
    withholdings, term,
        150, 165, 169
Taxable accounts, term, 162
Taxable interest, preparation, 163
Tax-advantaged accounts
    leveraging, 163–164
    money, withdrawal, 182
    term, 162, 176
Tax-advantaged giving,
        donor-advised fund
        (opening), 190–195
Tenants, search/screening, 126
Term life insurance, term, 222
Thrift Savings Plan (TSP), 27, 178
Ticker symbol, term, 37
Towing and labor cover-
        age, term, 218
Traditional IRAs, 23–26,
        163, 178, 198
    contribution eligibility,
        determination, 25
    term, 23–24, 176, 180, 184, 198
Transferable points, term, 60

TransUnion, credit report, 55
Travel hacker
    ability, determination, 61
    term, 59
Travel hacking, 59–63
    credit card, research/
        location, 61
Trinity Study, 14

U
Uninsured/underinsured motor-
        ist coverage, term, 217

V
Vanguard, 20, 24, 30, 39, 161,
        184, 192, 193, 198, 228

W
Wedding
    costs, control, 85–87
    off-season occurrence, 87
Wells Fargo, 20, 24, 30, 39, 161,
        184, 192, 198, 228
Whole life insurance, term, 222
Withdrawal rate
    determination, 182
    term, 180
Workplace retirement plan, 26
Work, quality (documentation),
        133